D0621957

A NEW KIND OF MAYOR

BREAKING THE MOLD

BILL MIRANDA

The contents of this book are based on actual experiences as recalled and/or investigated to the best ability of the author. Comments of a personal nature regarding any persons or organizations are the sole opinion of the author. No legal advice is intended.

No part of this publication may be reproduced, stored in a retrieval system, or transmitted in any form or by any means – electronic, mechanical, photocopy, recording, or otherwise – without prior written permission of the copyright owner.

Copyright © 2021 Bill Miranda
All rights reserved.
ISBN: 9781685244712

DEDICATION

Hundreds of people were involved in the making of my life's adventures, but only one was with me through the most exciting of them. From the first time I saw her, I knew my life would be a great adventure. What an adventure it's been. Virginia Norma Miranda, my precious and beloved wife, I dedicate this book to you because you not only helped me write it, but together we lived it. Thank you for being by my side every day in every way. Without you I am only another man.

With you, I am Da Mayor!

ACKNOWLEDGEMENTS

I could not have written this book without the influence and encouragement of many friends and relatives. So many people yet so little space to acknowledge them individually. Instead I will give a general shout out to all and a heartfelt thank you.

To produce this book, I called on the expertise of my good friends Judith Cassis (book writer extraordinaire) and Michael Asmar (photographer extraordinaire). The job of formatting went to Lynn Caprarelli (formatter extraordinaire). I thank them for their patience and understanding, for their expert counsel and most of all, for their love of this project.

FOREWORD

I once told Bill Miranda that if he were but to put pen to paper he could write anything, and those who love him would eat it up. But in true Bill Miranda style, he has exceeded expectations with A New Kind of Mayor. If you know Bill, you are aware of some of the WHATS about his life, and this new book offers an understanding of the WHYS.

I met Bill Miranda in 2009. My husband and I owned a local paper and Bill wrote weekly articles that educated and uplifted businesspeople. As an entrepreneur, I always looked forward to what he had to say.

Around that time Bill was also a business counselor with the SBDC. I signed up for business coaching to help me break through a challenge that held me back throughout my career, and I was grateful to tap into Bill's depth of knowledge and experience. There was one area in which I really needed help, and he honed in on it immediately.

Bill showed a sincere desire to help me succeed. I told him that even though I had built strong relationships in the

Santa Clarita business community I found it challenging to sell advertising for my paper—not because I didn't believe in the value of advertising, but because I had a hard time asking people for money.

Bill helped me to see that I was not asking for money, but offering solutions to people who were seeking answers. "Think of yourself as a doctor," Bill said. "People tell you where it hurts, you diagnose the problem and offer treatment."

I realized that being paid to provide my marketing services would not compromise my integrity. This paradigm shift allowed me to serve the businesses in our community on a whole different level. To this day I still use what Bill taught me.

Over the years, I've watched Bill's success unfold as he went from founding the Santa Clarita Valley Latino Chamber of Commerce to creating successful community events and ultimately allying with the Santa Clarita Chamber of Commerce. He joined the City Council in 2017, and at this writing, he sits as the first Latino Mayor of Santa Clarita.

Bill never followed the crowd. Ever. He sought the road less traveled and from there carved his own path. Others joined him along the way and Bill welcomed them, helping them to actualize their own successes.

These pages contain the memoirs of a man who broke through barriers that may otherwise have halted his progress. Throughout his life, Bill trampled the odds and kept on going.

A New Kind of Mayor chronicles the experiences that shaped Bill's character and solidified his values. His stories illustrate the trickle-down effect of strong leadership and the value of taking action in the face of adversity.

A New Kind of Mayor is his story. Motivated by a sense of purpose and a desire to make an impact, this book also shows ways in which Bill Miranda has made history. It was my pleasure to work with him on bringing it to fruition.

Judith Cassis, Book Coach and New York Times Bestselling Ghostwriter

www.judithcassis.com

TABLE OF CONTENTS

PREFACE

I'm a new kind of mayor in Santa Clarita. I am the first Latino and first person of color to serve as mayor of our city. I began by bringing a new perspective to the office of councilmember, and I've carried that momentum to the mayor's seat.

Although Santa Clarita has had mayors that supported multiculturalism, diversity, equity and inclusion, I am the first one who has lived a lifetime in each of those worlds.

I didn't just read about the civil rights movement of the '60s, I lived it. I had a conversation with the great Jackie Robinson and came face to face with the loathsome white supremist, George Wallace. I didn't just watch the news of the Cold War on television, I lived it. I was there when dozens of our nuclear bombers rolled down the runway in what we thought was the start of a nuclear war.

The subtitle of this book, *Breaking the Mold* is not intended to disrespect all of the great work of our prior mayors. On the contrary, I use the term to suggest enhancement of the mold. Santa Clarita is a great city. It is becoming more diverse every day. I represent the future; a future where we embrace multiculturalism, diversity, equity and inclusion; a future where all demographics, all beliefs, not only have a place at the table, but also have the ability to influence it.

I helped break the mold in the '70s when I worked for IBM and Xerox. Many corporate employers did not hire people of color to fill leadership positions at that time. While others of color, feeling they had no chance, didn't even bother to apply, I stayed and fought to create leadership positions. I wasn't just fighting for myself, but also for those who would follow. At times I fought alone. Sometimes I had allies. Either way, I was willing to risk it all to break the old mold.

Years later, having achieved measurable success as a business executive, I broke the mold again. I gave up a six-figure income, great benefits, and stock options, and I walked away from the "golden handcuffs" of the corporate world to form my own business. I did it my way. It was a roller coaster ride but it turned out to be an enjoyable and successful adventure.

Believe it or not, it was suffering a stroke near the height of my career that altered my trajectory. What did that mean for my future? And our family's future? After two years of recovering, ever grateful, I was back at it. Now I was trying to make a difference in the world, my world of Santa Clarita.

When I found Latinos in need of advocacy in our community, I broke the mold again by separating from the Santa Clarita Chamber of Commerce and forming the SCV Latino Chamber of Commerce. Now, twelve years later, Latinos have a seat at almost every table in our city. Sometimes, even when it goes against the grain, you have to break the mold to create a stronger one.

I'm White. I'm Black. I'm Mulatto. I'm Mestizo. I'm Latino. But mostly I'm American. In spite of all my trials and tribulations, I am a happy product of the American dream. Born to parents who migrated to the United States from Puerto Rico, I was raised in an eclectic barrio in New York City. I've been honed by my years in the military, enlightened by corporate giants IBM, Xerox, and Data General, and challenged by the many obstacles of entrepreneurship. Throughout it all I was on the leading edge of diversity, equity, and inclusion. I am proud to say America has been very, very good to me.

On January 17, 2017, I became the second Latino to take a seat on the Santa Clarita City Council. Being appointed to the seat was an important achievement, not just for myself, but also for those I represented. Santa Clarita, one of the largest cities in the country in population, was rapidly becoming an integrated multicultural community. Whites made up the largest portion of the city followed by Latinos, Asians and Blacks. All were becoming significant populations in our city. When you include Muslims, LGBTQ+, and Native Americans, Santa Clarita is on its way to becoming a melting pot of cultures, and that creates a better America for us all.

As I write this book, changes are occurring to move diversity, equity, and inclusion forward in Santa Clarita. Our congressional representative in Washington, D.C. is Mike Garcia, a Latino. Our State Assemblywoman is Suzette Martinez Valladares, a Latina. Our police chief is Justin Diez, also a Latino. Our fire chief is African American, Daryl Osby.

Our assistant City Manager is Frank Oviedo, a Latino and me, a different kind of mayor than Santa Clarita has ever had.

Economic vitality is also seeing changes. Business ownership and corporate management is becoming more and more diverse and our community is responding to it. The Board of Directors of the SCV Chamber of Commerce is more diverse than ever thanks to its excellent management team led by John Musella and Ivan Volschenk.

I am hopeful these significant strides will set a precedent for the future. Santa Clarita has always been a great place to live, work, play and raise a family. My family moved to Santa Clarita 38 years ago and it's been a wonderful experience raising our children here.

This book is a collection of my memoirs centering around the day I was appointed to the city council. I detail how I was selected over 50 competitors to fill the seat, what I did to prepare and what it was like. I chronicle my journey from the mean streets of New York to the mayor's seat in Santa Clarita.

This book is also a love story. It is the story of 47 years of marriage to my beautiful wife, Virginia. Our adventures extended far beyond those of most marriages and I share many of them here. Recently, my Virginia reminded me that I promised her the world when we got married and I delivered. I didn't deliver, Sweetheart. We delivered everything together.

Ultimately, I decided to write this book to inspire others to follow their dreams. Take adventurous journeys. Live great lives. Success is not what society dictates. Success is what you define it as. There was a time when I had more material things than I could ever use. But it wasn't until I found service to others that I truly became successful in my life. It is my sincere hope that my story inspires you and gives you the courage to be the one to break the mold in your world.

CHAPTER ONE

GAME DAY

January 17, 2017

It was game day. In the early afternoon I was finishing up last minute preparations for my run for City Council. I reread the council agenda for that evening. It read:

CITY COUNCIL VACANCY

On December 4, 2016, Mayor Pro Tem Dante Acosta created a vacancy on the City Council by resigning his seat on the City Council, as a result of his election as a Member of the California Legislature. At the regular meeting of December 13, 2016, the City Council approved a process to solicit applications from Santa Clarita residents interested in being appointed to the City Council. The City Council approved holding a special meeting on January 17, 2017 for purposes of considering candidates and potentially appointing a new member to serve on the City Council. RECOMMENDED ACTION: City Council receive report, consider candidate applications, hear candidate presentations, discuss, and appoint a new Member of the City Council to serve the remainder of the vacant term of office, currently set to expire on December 11, 2018.

I had completed and submitted my application to the city clerk two hours before the deadline. I had worked on my three-minute presentation for hours with my wife, Virginia. I felt I was ready to present passionately and flawlessly. I asked Virginia to rehearse with me again to make sure I had it right.

Virginia, my wife and "partner in crime," has been through all the wars with me. She is my biggest fan and my most important consigliere. When I approached her in December 2016, about applying for the council seat, we discussed the pros and cons for hours and decided to pray on it, asking for guidance. As spiritual people, we believe that His will is what will be done.

After praying for several days, we felt strongly that I should apply. We also decided that we would go through the appointment process together. Virginia helped me complete the application, get the references, and prepare for the required three-minute presentation. That afternoon she ran through my presentation with me for the final time.

She offered these final words of encouragement. "Remember your reason for applying. You have championed Latino causes all your life, including helping Dante with his campaign for the California State Assembly. We need Latino representation on the council and no one is more qualified and deserving of that seat than you. Tonight, stay focused and speak a bit faster than you're used to doing. Three minutes is a very short time to state all your qualifications. Focus on the most important ones and deliver them with the passion that's in your heart."

Virginia is the mildest, kindest, most caring person in the world, making her a perfect person to teach and coach others. She instills confidence in people yet ensures they stay on point. That was exactly what I needed. We went through the presentation together and were satisfied that I was ready. Virginia had some errands to run and suggested I get some rest while she was gone. I kissed her goodbye, sat alone in my favorite chair and drifted off a bit. I couldn't help thinking how far we'd come.

CHAPTER TWO

COMING HOME

In December 1981 my employer Data General sent me, along with my family, to live in Paris, France. After spending a marvelous year there, it was time to return home to Los Angeles. I had accepted an assignment to serve as the District Manager in Los Angeles. A friend from the Los Angeles area sent me a copy of the L.A. Times real estate section so we could get a jump on finding a place to live. While scanning through the pages, out jumped a bright, four-color ad. In big, bold type it shouted, Come Home to Valencia!

"Honey, you have to see this," I said to Virginia. "This could be just what we're looking for." Virginia read the ad out loud. As she shouted out each amenity, our excitement level rose. When she finished, we looked at each other and smiled, feeling pretty sure we had just stumbled upon Nirvana.

On Thursday, December 23, 1982, we arrived at LAX. Christmas was in the air and we were home. With a sigh of relief, Virginia and I, and our daughters Lisa, 14, and Eva, 6, arrived at the terminal building. The energy was palpable and everyone seemed to be smiling. I marveled as I watched my girls walk in and out of shops, thrilled to experience life in their native language and customs again. Mother and daughters were chattering away, clearly happy to be home.

"Sweetheart," Virginia called out, a bright smile on her face. "I want to call my parents in Sacramento to let them know we've arrived back in the good ole U.S. of A." And with that, she blew me a kiss, and was off to phone her parents.

It was just two days before Christmas, and because of the move, Virginia and I hadn't had time to Christmas shop. We figured once we got to the hotel, we would work out a plan. I was feeling good and thinking that maybe we could take the girls shopping with us and make it a family shopping affair. I was relishing our return home and imagining a great Christmas together. Then I saw Virginia slowly walking toward me with tears in her eyes. "I just called my parents. Mother said I need to fly up to Sacramento right away. Daddy just found out that he has cancer." Her voice was soft as she struggled to say those words to me.

Christmas Eve morning, after a sleepless night of crying with and comforting Virginia, I put her and Eva on a plane to Sacramento, and then put Lisa on another plane to visit her sister in Cincinnati. I was left alone to start my new assignment as Data General's district manager. I also had to find a house, buy a car, and Christmas shop for the kids. But I was determined to do those things. It was important for Virginia to be with her parents during that difficult time.

My hotel was on Flower Street in downtown L.A. There were several car dealerships within walking distance of the hotel so I headed out on foot. By mid-afternoon, after test-driving a handful of cars, we were the proud owners of a brand new 1983 Honda Accord. I parked the car in the hotel garage and walked over to my new office on 7th and Flower. I was welcomed warmly by my teammates. They told me my position had been vacant for several months and many decisions and actions were awaiting my arrival. They hoped I would hit the ground running so we could start the new year on the right foot. I mentioned that I was living in a hotel and had to find a place for my family and me to live. I had two girls to get into school and the new year was starting in just over a week. I promised to be as involved as I could with the team but asked their indulgence as I got settled in. There was an air of disappointment in the room. Welcome back to L.A. Bill.

I was worried about Virginia's father. Armand Bidabe was 66-years-old and just a year retired from his work as an electrician for Douglas Aircraft. He and Virginia's mother, Lilly, were married 42 years. He was a hardworking man who enjoyed life to the fullest even when it didn't go as planned and had come to the United States as a 14-year-old from Cananea, Mexico. He survived as a young man by working in the silver mines in Bisbee, Arizona and Tehachapi, California, and had mined gold in Jackson, California.

It was in Jackson in 1940 that he met Lilly. Shortly thereafter they eloped. He was 24 and she was 19. They didn't have much, but they had each other. Things moved fast for the couple in the early '40s. Baby Gloria was born in 1941, Armand was drafted into the army in 1943, and Virginia was born in 1944. Armand, who had saved much of his military pay, was able to put a down payment on a tiny house in Jackson that sold for $1,000. The family lived there for 12 years until Armand decided his two daughters should have more opportunities in life than what was offered in the small town of Jackson. He accepted a job with Douglas Aircraft in Santa Monica and moved the family there in 1956.

Armand worked at Douglas Aircraft for 25 years. He retired in 1981, longing to return to the quiet life in Jackson. However, property values in Jackson had climbed far above what his retirement pay would allow, so he bought a house in nearby Sacramento. A year later he was diagnosed with lung cancer. This type of cancer was later traced to his job at Douglas working around asbestos.

Virginia called later Christmas Eve night. "Daddy is not doing well," she said. "He's despondent and in pain. He needs me. Mother needs me, too. I know it's asking a lot of you, but I need you to bring me some of my things on Sunday. Then I need you to take Eva back to Los Angeles with you."

It was Friday. "Of course, but why don't I just come in the morning," I asked.

"No," she replied. "Daddy is not wanting visitors right now, even though you are family. Stay there, go to mass and pray really hard for daddy. I love you, my Sweetheart." And with that, we gave each other a virtual hug and hung up.

Saturday, Christmas day, I got up early, ate a hearty breakfast and went to mass. I prayed extra hard, especially for Armand. I spent the day alone walking the streets of downtown with only my feelings to ponder. It was not the Christmas I had hoped for 48 hours earlier.

Sunday, I got up early. I decided to drive the brand new Honda to Sacramento. Having been an outside salesman for many years, I always found being on the road alone with my thoughts very relaxing. I really needed to relax. I was worried for Armand, Lilly, and Virginia. After six hours on the road, I arrived at the Bidabe home in Sacramento. I rang the doorbell and heard little steps running to the front door. It was Eva, squealing with delight. "It's Daddy!"

Virginia opened the door and gave me a great big hug. I knew immediately that she was clinging to me in hopes her turmoil would go away. I picked up Eva, kissed her and grabbed Virginia's hand. She walked us to the bedroom where Lilly sat bedside near Armand. I hadn't seen either of them in two years. Now, not knowing how I should react, I forced a smile and said hello to both of them. Lilly stood up and gave me a warm hug. I could tell she had spent many days crying, and that she had worked hard to make Armand as comfortable as she could. Armand waved to me from his bed. He said he was sorry I had to come so far just because of him. His voice was weak. He looked much thinner than I remembered. How could a big strong man like Armand be reduced to that? I wanted to cry but knew I shouldn't.

After a few hours, I said my goodbyes, packed Eva in the car, and headed back to L.A. It only took six hours to get back to the hotel but it felt like six days. I knew I had many challenges ahead, but it was nothing compared to the weight Virginia and her family were carrying.

First, I had to find a place to live and get the girls in school while trying to do my job. Finding a place to live was not as difficult as I thought it would be. Remember Come Home to Valencia? I looked at about 40 homes there before I narrowed it down to three possibilities.

Eva had been staying with my brother. On Friday morning, New Year's Eve, I picked her up and we made the journey back to Sacramento. I showed Virginia the housing options and together we chose the house we still live in today. She told me not to worry about colors, carpets or drapes. "When I get to see it, I'll probably want to change them all anyway." She paused a moment before adding, "I'm sorry I can't be more helpful to you. I just can't leave right now and maybe not for weeks or even months. I know I'm asking a lot, but I just can't leave my parents now. They both need me."

We had a quiet New Year's Eve together. Lily cooked a hearty Mexican breakfast before Eva and I headed back to L.A. I still felt terrible about Armand, but the drive home passed quickly. My thoughts were filled with things I needed to accomplish in the week ahead.

During the time between New Year's Day and early June, the girls and I were busy bees. Once I'd put a deposit down on the house in Valencia, I knew where to enroll the kids in school. Lisa was enrolled in Placerita Junior High and Eva in Meadows Elementary. I arranged for Eva to be picked up from school by an after-school daycare service called Town & Country Farm School. I picked her up every day by 6 p.m. Then I'd take the girls to dinner before helping them with their homework and putting them to bed.

I did my best while Virginia was away. Lisa was a stellar athlete at Placerita and played basketball and softball.

Coming to a new school mid-year from another country had to be incredibly difficult, especially with her mother being away. Even though Virginia visited us several times during those months, it wasn't the same as having her with us every day. Eva adjusted the best. She made many new friends and even wanted me to sign her up for little league.

Besides having to juggle so many balls, I felt a deep sense of loss at work. Gone was the joie de vivre I had enjoyed while working in Europe. Gone was the small company feel that had given way to the suits on Wall Street. In my heart, I knew I wasn't long for the corporate world. Somehow, I was able to perform moderately well in my job and moderately well at home. Neither was at the standard I had always set for myself, but this was a different situation. I was used to having Virginia by my side. She wasn't there and I felt like I was a lesser person because of it. I was also an exhausted person. But no more so than she. She was physically and emotionally drained. Then it happened.

Saturday morning, June 11, 1983, my girls and I were getting ready for Eva's baseball game when the phone rang. It was Virginia. I answered it pretty much knowing what I was about to hear. I was right. "He's gone. Daddy is gone. I held his hand as he left us." She was tearful, but not crying her normal cry. This cry was one of total exhaustion, a cry of surrendering to the inevitable, a cry of hopelessness.

"I'm so sorry," I said holding back my own tears. "I'll come up with girls to help with the arrangements. I love you, Sweetheart."

"I love you, too, Darling," came her soft and somewhat distant reply.

We buried Armand in his beloved Jackson. The ceremony was modest with only a few dozen close friends and family in attendance. Virginia and I convinced her mother, Lilly, to move in with us in Valencia. Lilly is a very independent woman. Convincing her was not easy, but under the circumstances it was the most logical thing to do. Thus, by summer our family was reunited and we could live somewhat normal lives in our new community of Valencia. Who would have thought that 38 years later Valencia would be part of the City of Santa Clarita, and I would be its mayor.

CHAPTER THREE

LIVING IN THE HEIGHTS

Arriving at the Council Chamber

It was almost 5:00 p.m., January 17, 2017. There was not an empty seat in the Santa Clarita City Council Chamber except one. That one, up on the dais, was the vacant city council seat that 51 of us wanted to win. I sat in the front row of the chamber awaiting the start of one of the most memorable council meetings in Santa Clarita history.

I looked around and saw many people I knew in attendance. There were former elected officials, medical professionals, educators, business leaders, and many other concerned citizens who wanted to step up and serve our great city. It was exciting to see so many candidates. And it was daunting. Imagine, 51 candidates for only one seat.

As I looked around, I saw two men I knew sitting close by, who were active members of the community and certainly deserving of consideration for the appointment. Near them were a current and a former elected official both of whom also deserved serious consideration. A good friend, renowned for helping seniors in our community both professionally and with advocacy, was in attendance and had also applied. Surely he was deserving of consideration. And there were many others.

There were also many people I'd never seen before, and I found that to be very strange. I had been active in our community for almost 30 years and had no idea who they were. I was a Rotarian, board member of the Santa Clarita Valley Chamber of Commerce, active with seniors, veterans, the homeless, and women's organizations, yet I didn't know many of the candidates in the room. I asked myself why people would apply to be on the council without truly knowing the ins and outs of our community. Since the only qualifications to apply were that you had to live within the city's borders, offer three references, and make a three-minute presentation to the city council, I guessed pretty much anyone could apply. As it turned out, several of them presented very well and ended up being formidable competitors right to the end.

I sat next to a young candidate. She was an educator with young children. She told me she didn't know all that the job of a councilmember entailed, but she was willing to learn and put her heart into it. She knew it was a long shot but her heart led her to try. I told her I was impressed that she was willing to put herself out there and do whatever was needed to serve our community. In fact, I was impressed that 51 of us were willing to do that.

People were greeting one another, waving to one another across the room, and wishing them good luck. The pressure was on and everyone was trying not to think about their upcoming presentations. The packed house just made everyone's anxiety worse.

As I waited for the meeting to start, my mind drifted to my childhood and growing up in the inner city.

Mami & Papi

I grew up in New York City. My parents each migrated there from Puerto Rico in the '30s. My mother's name was Ermelinda, but everyone called her Linda. My father's name

19

was Guillermo, but everyone called him William. To me they were Mami and Papi.

Mami and Papi met in New York City and fell madly in love almost immediately. Papi was just 18-years-old. Mami was 29 and divorced with two little ones. My brother Eddie was 5 at the time and my sister, Linda, was 4. I try to imagine what it was like when my father told his mother he wanted to marry Ermelinda. Imagine having your 18-year-old son come to you saying, "I've met the woman of my dreams and I want to marry her." Deep breath. "Oh, and by the way, she's 29 and she's divorced." That might fly today, but in 1942 it didn't fly at all. I can almost hear his mother's gasp. And before she can recover, he adds, "Did I mention she has two little kids?

Somehow, and I don't know how, my father was able to convince her that nothing, especially common sense, was going to change his mind. The marriage took place in September 1942. Knowing my mother, I'd be willing to bet she charmed grandma and the rest of the Miranda family so completely that they fell in love with her and joyfully blessed the union.

With barely a penny to his name, my 18-year-old father ventured into the unknown world of fatherhood and being a husband. A few months later my mother discovered she was pregnant with me, and soon after my father was drafted into the army. Six months later he was on his way to war in the Pacific.

When he returned home three years later, he was amazed at how my mother had handled things in his absence.

Times were tough financially but Mami always figured things out. She was very good at survival. Now Papi was back. Things had to get better.

The first thing my father had to do was find work. With all the veterans returning it was very hard. He was now an unemployed, married, 22-year-old father of three. My mother prayed everyday asking the Lord to provide a job for her husband, and the Lord provided. My father landed a job in the restaurant of the Commodore Hotel in Grand Central Station. He worked as a bus boy and as a substitute waiter. His brother-in-law was a waiter there and gave my father a glowing reference. Without ever having been a waiter in his life, my Papi became a substitute waiter at one of the finest restaurants in New York City. To his credit he handled the job very well. The hourly pay wasn't much, but the tips were great. We were still poor, but at least we could eat and pay the rent.

Grammar School Years

My grammar school years were great for me. I made good friends, played lots of games, and had good teachers.

We all have our favorites and mine were Mrs. David in the 4th grade and Mrs. Finkel in the 6th. They're both in heaven right now watching me very closely. I'm sure of it.

Mrs. David was a retired teacher who substituted on occasion. She had beautiful white hair, wore fancy reading glasses, and had a soft-spoken elegance about her. She was also considered the meanest teacher in school. My regular 4th grade teacher, Mrs. Holman, fell off a horse and due to her injuries wouldn't be returning for several months. Enter Mrs. David. I was scared stiff. I'd heard of her reputation. One day during reading Mrs. David called on me. I was barely an average reader at the time and she demanded excellence. I wasn't at that level. I read the passage well but hesitated for long periods between sentences. Mrs. David asked me to read it again. I was mortified. I read it again just as I had before.

Mrs. David said, "Willie, your reading is very good. Just try not to hesitate before each sentence. Now read it again without the pauses." I read it a third time without the pauses.

"Very good," she said. "You can be a very special reader. You just have to keep working at it."

With that boost in confidence and much more encouragement from her, I went on to become an exceptional reader and student. All it took was the insistence that I do it right and a pat on the back. I carried that lesson with me throughout my entire career. Insist on excellence and give pats on the back freely. Thank you, Mrs. David. You changed my life.

Mrs. Finkel was my 6th grade teacher. Like Mrs. David, she demanded a level of excellence from those students she felt could achieve it. Entering her class, I considered myself a very good student and had become quite the confident kid. I was good in sports, good at games, socially adept and a good citizen. There were, however, a few things I was not good at. For instance, being fully committed to my studies and dressing for success. Mrs. Finkel fixed the commitment part. She consistently challenged me and never let me slough off. The clothing part wasn't so easy. I had to wear my brother's clothes and they hung on me dreadfully. At first, I was embarrassed by it. Then I just accepted the fact that we were poor. Not destitute, just poor.

There was, however, one time Mrs. Finkel crossed the line with me. It was recess. I was on the basketball court struggling to make a shot. Mrs. Finkel blew her whistle. Everybody stopped and stared as she walked over to me, grabbed the ball from my hands, and in her high heels shot the ball into the basket.

"See," she said. "How hard is that?"

I'd be willing to bet that if she tried making that shot 100 times, she couldn't do it again.

After a year of Mrs. Finkel challenging me, and with her guidance, I succeeded academically and was placed in a special progress class going into junior high. I finished the 7th, 8th, and 9th grades in only two years. I owe both women a great deal especially since they helped to lay a good foundation of education for my life.

Good Supportive Family

My parents were in love and showed it often. Family was everything to them. They had to struggle most of their lives to raise us, pay the bills, and put food on the table. My mother was a very loving and caring person and I couldn't have asked for better. She had a great personality and was well liked by everybody. At the same time, she was a disciplinarian and a no nonsense person. It was her way or the highway. "This is what you're going to do, this is how you're going to do it. You can whine and complain all you want, but when you're done whining and complaining, you're going to do as I say."

And that's what we did.

My father was also a loving and caring person. He was my idol growing up. He spoke perfect Spanish and by the time I reached junior high he was fluent in English as well. He was handsome and always had a smile on his face.

Always an optimist, he often told me, "Son, you can be anything you want to be. You can do anything you want to do. Opportunity is everywhere. All you have to do is seek it out. All you have to do is focus. You can do it. Focus."

Whenever I struggled with something, it was his advice I sought.

"Son," he'd say. "Nothing's easy until you learn how to do it. Keep working at it. Get better. Soon you will be really good at it. Don't ever give up. Figure it out and stay focused."

My sister Linda was five years older and was more like another mother to me. She picked me up from school, took me to the park, made me snacks, dressed me and took me to  church. Linda attended Catholic schools K-12. She was a lady, well educated, and of very good character. She loved to dance, and with my brother Eddie as her partner, competed and won several local dance contests. She also won a beauty contest. She married, had two boys, and worked for many years at Saks Fifth Avenue. She retired from the U.S. Post Office. She passed away from breast cancer in her sixties. I loved and respected her so much. God bless her soul.

My brother Eddie was always looking out for his little brother. If anybody messed with me, they would have to mess with him, and he was a pretty tough kid. Eddie was an excellent baseball player who played semi-pro in New York. He joined the army in his late teens and retired years later as a master sergeant. He worked for Amtrak for many years and retired from that, too. He married, had children, and is retired and living a quiet life in New Jersey. Eddie always had the most incredible work ethic. Even as a child, he found ways to earn money by working. Whether it was helping ladies carry their groceries home from the market or shining shoes on the streets, Eddie never shied away from hard work. Whenever I got a bit lazy in life, I

just thought about Eddie. Then I would suck it up and do whatever had to be done. Thank you, my brother.

My little sister Millie, four years younger than I, was my "partner in crime" growing up. We had many adventures that were fun to us but would have scared the heck out of our parents had they known. Whether it was collecting empty bottles from the street gutters for the deposit money or borrowing a bicycle and riding it together miles away from home, Millie was a trooper. She never squealed on me. Millie attended public school K-6 then Catholic School 7-12. She married, had two wonderful kids, graduated from college, and retired after many years working as the registrar at Saint Thomas Aquinas College in New York. She and her husband Bill, a retired New York Police officer, are enjoying their retirement with their four grandkids.

I'm very proud of my younger sister. She was a mother of two little ones when she decided to go back to finish college. She worked her tail off while attending night school, got her bachelor's degree, and interviewed for the registrar's position. When she was told the job required a master's degree, she sold herself so well that she got the job without meeting that requirement. She got her master's degree years later when she really didn't need it anymore. She showed she was more than up for the job.

Bill and Millie Today

Being Around Good People

Whether by design or luck I've always surrounded myself with good people. My first school friends were three African American boys named Michael Strong, Joseph Eason, and Bobby Bell. We were in first grade together. One day after school, Michael walked up to me and asked if I wanted to play with him on the playground. I said okay and soon after that Joseph joined us and then Bobby. Mr. Bell, Bobby's father, who always wore a  suit and tie, watched over us. As much as I enjoy thinking about my times with the boys, I mostly remember Mr. Bell, his suit, and tie. Someday when I grew up, I thought maybe I could wear a suit and tie just like his.

Peter Weissman and I became best friends in second grade. When we first met his name was Peter Warden. His family was German-Jewish and had barely escaped the Holocaust of World War II. They changed their name to Warden in order to escape the Nazi's and eventually immigrated to the United States and settled in New York. Some kids in class liked to tease him about being Jewish and make him cry. I hated that. One day I did something about it. I walked up to one of the bullies and pushed him hard. He fell backward and started to cry. They never teased Peter in front of me again.

Peter and I became the best of friends. He taught me to play chess and we played a lot of it. He beat me 50 straight games or so, but I've always had a competitive edge to me that said, "Sooner or later, I'm going to beat this guy." And then one day I did. Never mind that I ended up losing the next 50 games because he liked to win too. Eventually, we each won our fair share of matches. I truly believe playing chess helped me to improve academically. It exercised my mind and helped me to focus. I learned to think ahead and to strategize, and that has proven invaluable throughout my life. Thank you, Peter Weissman, for your friendship and the gift of chess.

I met Oscar Montalvo in the third grade. One day at recess, "super-shy" Oscar asked me if I would ask the teacher for a ball to play. I went and got the ball for him and we became great friends. That friendship still remains today.

In New York City in the early '50s baseball was ingrained in most New Yorkers. Oscar and I were no exception. We not only had three baseball teams, the Giants, Dodgers, and Yankees, we had three great baseball teams. From 1949 to 1956, it was one of the New York teams that won the World Series. Many times, it ended up being two of the New York teams facing off for the championship. It was our very own Field of Dreams. In the spring, Oscar and I played baseball, weather permitting. When it didn't permit, we played imaginary baseball in his family's cramped apartment.

Oscar lived on one of the toughest streets in a rough neighborhood. That he was able to avoid becoming a gang member or an addict is a wonderful tribute to his character. Sports, and later music, kept him from succumbing to the pressures of the streets. What kept me out of trouble: baseball and chess.

In my family, baseball was more than just a game. I vividly recall a night in 1955. I was in my room doing homework and my parents were watching a baseball game on TV in the living room. Suddenly there came shouts and screams from the living room. "Willie! Willie! Come here quick. Hurry." I ran out of my room, frightened by what I might see. As I bolted into the living room my parents were standing up pointing at the TV and jumping and shouting, "Roberto Clemente! Roberto Clemente! He's Puerto Rican! Willie, he's Puerto Rican!"

Symbols are important in life. Roberto Clemente was the first Puerto Rican Major League Baseball star. Being the first meant so much to our people. Jackie Robinson was the first African American Major League Baseball player. He, too, was an important symbol to his people. What's even more important is the fact that both were men of exemplary character that strived to help others.

A couple of years later Jackie Robinson spoke at my junior high graduation. He spoke for 30 minutes. Afterwards,

I was able to shake his hand. Jackie Robinson was a tremendous human being who stood up for his dignity in college, in the military, in baseball, and in society.

Stitt Junior High School

In the fall of 1955, I entered Stitt Junior High School as a 7th grader. I was in a special progress class and on track to complete the 7th, 8th, and 9th grades in two years. Unfortunately, the special class was made up mostly of nerdy students (except me of course), and I was placed at a school where they hated nerds. The students took one look at us when we arrived and said, "Special? You're not special in this school."

To prove we weren't special, they really made those two years tough on us. The very first day of school a bunch of bullies approached me and asked to see my bus pass. I asked why and the leader repeated, "I SAID I want to SEE your bus pass." I gave him my bus pass to see. He didn't even look at it. He just put it in his pocket and sneered. "Now that's much better," he said as he walked away. Bus passes were issued to us on the first school day of each month.

Coincidentally, Mr. Bully visited me on those days like clockwork. After a few months, Mr. Bully and I became close. Our ritual went something like this. "Hello, Mr. Bully. How are

you today? That's good to hear. Oh, so you don't have to kick my a$$ today, here's my bus pass and thank you for your kindness."

He graduated after that first year and I was relieved to know I wouldn't have to deal with him anymore. But a second bully tried to fill the void and do the same routine on me. This one wanted my lunch pass. That's where I drew the line. "You better get out of my face," I yelled. "You ain't getting crap from me. Now move out the way before my boys get here and move you."

It was pure bluff, but it worked. My second year at Stitt I became a different boy. I was bigger, stronger and more willing to fight off bullies rather than give in. Once, I even got into a short fight with Frankie Lyman at school. Yes, Frankie Lyman, the '50s rock and roll star known for his hit song, Why Do Fools Fall in Love. One day, I was scuttling down the hallway to my class. Frankie was coming toward me from the opposite direction. Unexpectedly, he opened a door and it slammed into my face. Words and blows were exchanged but a passing teacher stopped the bout. I don't normally hold a grudge, but I never bought another Frankie Lyman record after that.

When the school year ended I was thrilled. I had survived Stitt. I wondered if I'd survive high school even though I was smarter and more streetwise. I dreamed of becoming a professional baseball player. At my graduation, guest speaker Jackie Robinson offered this advice.

"I know many of you like baseball. I know you want to become major leaguers. I have some advice for you. The odds of anyone becoming a major league baseball player are so small you can't even imagine them. Stay in school. Get a college degree when you get older. The odds of being successful with a college degree are much greater. It doesn't matter how good of a baseball player you are."

I took that to heart. I gave baseball its due, but my main focus became getting through high school and getting a college degree. Jackie ended his speech with this: "The most luxurious possession, the richest treasure anybody has, is his personal dignity."

The Inner City

Life outside of Stitt wasn't all that great either. We lived on the sixth floor of a six-story building. The roof above us was a hangout for druggies. Our apartment had locks upon locks on top of locks. The apartment window leading to the fire escape even had locks on it to keep people out. If a fire happened, there was no escaping through the fire escape, but my parents were more worried about keeping the bad guys out.

Our biggest challenge was using the elevator. When the elevator door opened, I looked to see if anyone was in it.

If there was I didn't get in. If there wasn't, I got in and hoped it didn't stop along the way to the sixth floor.

The neighborhood streets, especially at night, didn't offer much in the way of safety either. Gangs controlled some of the streets and druggies controlled the rest. Only the main thoroughfares like Broadway were safe. The streets of New York were called mean streets for good reason. There was a lot of meanness out there. Almost every day, someone got robbed, beat up, or even killed. The police tried to control things, but they couldn't get a grip on them because no one would talk to them. Talking to the cops was looked upon as snitching and snitching would get you in a world of hurt.

My father introduced me to the public library when I was nine and got me a library card. Reading in the library was much easier than trying to read at home. I loved the library. It was safe. It was comfortable, and the books were fun to read. The library gave me sanctuary as a kid. It also opened my eyes to the world I had yet to explore. To this day, I visit the library regularly.

Summer of '57

I left Stitt with a warning from one of the gangs. We'll see you in high school. Because I refused to back down most of the time my last year at Stitt, I had been in a number of fistfights. I won more than I lost, but at Stitt that came with a price. The boy culture at Stitt was win a fight, make enemies. Lose a fight, make more enemies. Either way you lost. I had too many enemies now whose threats against me were very real. I was a little afraid of going to the local high school because of it. I considered skipping town. I was still pondering the decision mid-summer when I heard some shocking news. The same gang that threatened me had caught up with another kid, 15-year-old Michael Farmer. They trapped him at the local swimming pool where 20 of them took turns beating and stabbing him until he died. When I heard that, I decided there was no way I was going to school with them. Instead, I went in search of Dick and Jane.

For those unfamiliar with Dick and Jane, they were the main characters in my second grade reader aptly titled, Fun with Dick and Jane. Dick and Jane lived with their parents in the suburbs, in a wonderful house, with a white picket fence.

They lived with little sister Sally, their dog Spot, and their cat Puff. They were all wonderfully happy people. It was Mayberry RFD before Mayberry RFD.

I read about them in school and then went home. Dick and Jane were not there. The house with the white picket fence was not there. I went home to a tenement apartment. To get there I had to walk dangerous streets, dark corridors, and try to avoid bullies, druggies, and robbers. In the summer of 1957 I was sick of it and I wanted to go find Dick and Jane. I wanted to find that house with the white picket fence. I wanted to see Spot and Puff and Dick and Jane and Sally and their mom and dad, and their grandma and grandpa. Those are the people I wanted to see. But first I had to find them. So I set out to do just that.

I told my parents I was going off to a baseball camp for a couple of weeks and that I would be under adult supervision. I'm not sure they believed me, but I was allowed to go. I left home and hitchhiked part of the way across the country. I worked on horse farms. I shoveled manure, pitched hay, painted fences, ate grub and slept in barns. I never found Dick and Jane, but I made up my mind that I wasn't going back to school in New York City.

When summer ended, I returned home and told my parents about my fears of attending the high school. My father said a military school would be good for me, but money was too tight. My mother was determined I should be in a safe environment and she somehow convinced my father that they would find a way to pay for it. It became an extended family project where every aunt, uncle, cousin, and close family friend was asked to pitch in to "save Willie." With the full support of our extended family, my parents were able to pay for military school. I was grateful for all the support and vowed to work hard and make everyone proud of me.

CHAPTER FOUR

THERE CAN ONLY BE ONE

Fifty-one candidates waited impatiently to deliver presentations to the council. We were called to present in the same order that the city clerk had received the applications. Having just made the deadline by a couple of hours, I knew I would be one of the last to present. It was going to be a long night.

Mayor Cameron Smyth banged the gavel softly to begin the meeting. He asked Mayor Pro Tem Laurene Weste to lead us in the pledge of allegiance, which she did with a touch of patriotic fervor. As a veteran myself, I really like when someone delivers the pledge with patriotic fervor. When the pledge was done, everyone took their seats awaiting the Mayor's introductory comments.

He said some kind words about how impressed he was with the quantity and quality of the candidates being considered. He explained the process leading to the appointment. He added that if the council voted a candidate in that evening, he or she would take office in one week. If the council did not reach a decision that evening, the meeting would reconvene to continue the process the next day until a selection was made. He asked for comments from the other councilmembers prior to the start of presentations. Each councilmember, in turn, including Mayor Pro Tem Weste and councilmembers Marsha McLean and Bob Kellar, commented on how happy, proud, and amazed they were that 51 citizens cared enough about our city to go through the full application process.

I was sitting in the front row directly in front of the empty seat up on the dais. I had been in council chambers before, but this time was different. I was nervous and I was alone. Virginia wanted to join me, but I asked her not to come. I didn't want her to have to endure the hours of anxiety the meeting would cause her. After my insistence and some contemplation, she agreed to stay home.

Mayor Smyth quoted The Highlander when he said, "There can be only one." The candidates looked around nervously, trying to guess who would be the one. We smiled at one another even as the Mayor's words hit us all deeply, "There can be only one." I flashed back to a time when I was the only one, way back in military school.

Bordentown Military Institute

Entering Bordentown Military Institute as an inner city boy and a 14-year-old 10th grader was complete culture shock to me. I went from a school where everybody looked like me, or almost like me, to a school where nobody looked like me. The young cadets were white, mostly from financially well-off families, and they were older, bigger, and more experienced at being cadets. After my first week, I wasn't sure I could last a second one. I didn't see how I could ever adapt well enough to be accepted by the other cadets.

Entering the Cadet Corps at that time was a rough transition for me, but not just because I was Latino. I had come from an unstructured environment as an inner city kid to the extremely structured environment of military life. Suddenly, there was a right way to dress, walk, eat, and sleep. Every evening we formed our battalion, companies, and platoons in the courtyard. After an in-ranks inspection, we marched into chapel services where we sang hymns and heard inspirational talks from faculty members. Then we marched to the dining hall where we said grace before each meal. Meals were very formal and not social gatherings. It was completely foreign to me.

I couldn't seem to get anything right those first few weeks. I didn't know how to march and someone was constantly yelling at me to get it right. When I sat down to eat, more yelling for me to get it right. When my uniforms arrived, I thought I looked great in them, but more yelling at me to wear them right. I wasn't used to shining my shoes, certainly not every day. If I didn't shine my shoes daily, I got gigged. A gig meant you had to walk a penalty tour, which consisted of you marching back and forth in the courtyard for an hour. Those first few weeks the courtyard and I became pretty friendly. Why? Because I didn't shine my shoes. Old habits are hard to break.

The first year I helped to pay my way at school by washing dishes for 50 cents after every meal. It was a very humbling experience. I was a cadet learning to be an officer and a gentleman. Dine with dignity, then go wash the dishes.

No matter, it helped pay my way. I was not only helping myself, but I was helping my parents and my family.

I got into a few fights because some didn't like the idea of having a dark skinned Latino in the school. However, the great majority of the cadets received me well and were quite supportive. The faculty was fantastic and I must mention two of them whose influence has endured my entire life.

Dr. Harold Morrison Smith was the headmaster of the school. He believed academic excellence was the most important mission of the school. The military aspect was secondary. He was a powerful speaker who repeatedly reminded us that we were becoming the future leaders of America. Future leaders of America? Me? Wow. In addition to inspiring me, he helped my parents structure tuition, as well as room and board payments, to make them somewhat affordable. I recall one time when my father had fallen behind on payments, Dr. Smith asked us both into his office. I was afraid he was going to drop me from the school. Instead, he told my father that he understood the payments were too much for us and he gave us a grant to get us through the year. I am forever grateful for his generosity.

Marvin O. Borst was a basketball and baseball coach as well as an economics teacher. He was also my house faculty member my first two years at BMI. We never discussed it, but he was the one who ran interference for me with the Cadet Corps. He told some of the football players to watch over me should anyone try to bully me. Mr. Borst was a visionary. He inspired me with stories of people who achieved great success after coming from humble beginnings. As an athletic coach, he was one of the most competitive coaches I knew. No, he was not a screamer or chair thrower. He was always under control and always a gentleman. He just had a passion for winning and he knew how to make it happen.

My second year at BMI, I was promoted to the rank of sergeant in the Cadet Corps and that gave me a taste of serving in a leadership position. It was a good experience for the most part, however, those who struggled with having a Latino in the school, sure as heck didn't like it when one was telling them what to do. That led to angst in a few people. It caused some pushing and shoving, and in some cases, fist fighting. It happens, even in military school.

My senior year, I became a real cadet leader. I became the adjutant of the Cadet Corps. I was third in command of the entire corps. I had a real leadership position. When I joined military school, I was 5' tall, 100 pounds. By my senior year, I was almost 6' tall, 150 pounds. It's easy to pick on the little guy when he's new to the school, but it's a little harder to mess with a big guy when he's been in the school three years and is in a leadership position. That year went so much smoother.

I played a little basketball at school. One day while we were warming up before basketball practice, the Commandant of Cadets, Colonel John Roosma, walked into the gym wearing his military uniform. He was over 50 years old, but still tall and fit. He walked over to me and asked if he could take a few shots.

"Sure," I told him, and handed him the ball at the free throw line.

He took three shots and missed all three. "I'm getting too old," he said. Then he thanked me and walked off the court.

I watched him walk away and thought, "There's a guy who just tried to relive his high school days." It was sad.

Years later, I visited the Basketball Hall of Fame in Springfield, Massachusetts. Guess who is inducted there? Johnny Roosma of West Point. Yes, the same Colonel John Roosma. I learned an important lesson. Never pre-judge people. Many of the most talented people you meet have much to brag about. They just don't do it.

I walked into BMI an inner city kid with little knowledge of the world outside of my environment. I walked out of BMI a well-educated gentleman with the tools to become a leader in the real world.

Thank you, Dr. Smith, Mr. Borst, Mrs. Elizabeth Smith, Mr. Hartpence, Mr. Lytel and the many outstanding faculty members that made BMI a great place to learn. And most importantly, thank you Danny Larusso, Bobby Constantino, Pete Passaro, Rick Shippen, and the many other cadets that welcomed me and helped me through what were three of the best years of my life.

Patricia

My senior year of high school I dated a pretty, young lady named Patricia who lived in my neighborhood in New York. We saw each other about one weekend a month when I traveled to New York to visit my parents. She was 14 and I was 16. She was white, half Irish and half Finnish. Nobody was happy we were dating. Not her parents, not my parents, and not even our friends. No one thought we were a good fit. Except for us.

It started as puppy love, but by the end of a year it was more than that. When I entered the Air Force in January 1961, we were in love. We were married on her 18th birthday in March, 1963 and had our first little girl, Christine, on January 1, 1964. Patricia was still 18 and I was 20. Four years later we had our second little girl, Lisa. Three years later we were divorced.

Patricia and I had been having issues in our relationship, and we felt that a new environment would help. It didn't. We got to the point where we just couldn't live together anymore. We separated and eventually divorced.

Sadly, Patricia passed away 23 years later in a tragic car accident. I was sorry for the hurt I had caused her and I pray for her often. I gave the eulogy at her burial. She was the mother of two of my daughters and she deserves my gratitude and prayers.

My daughter Christine grew up to become a wonderful young lady. She grew up mostly with her mother in Cincinnati, Ohio where Patricia moved with her second husband. Christine attended the University of Cincinnati where she met Mr. Right. Andrew is an architect. They both graduated from the University of Cincinnati and live in Cincinnati as do the eldest three of my six wonderful grandchildren. My grandson Jackson is a schoolteacher and an athletic coach in the Cincinnati school system. Granddaughter Elena is a recent graduate of Kenyon College in Ohio where she captained the women's basketball team. Granddaughter Lauren is killing it in high school right now, academically and athletically.

My daughter Lisa lives with us here in Santa Clarita. She attended Hart High, graduated from the College of the Canyons where she played basketball, and graduated from

California State University Northridge. She works for Mercury Insurance as a claims adjuster. She has worked there for many years and does very well. She is content living with us and we're content having her.

My youngest daughter is Eva. She graduated from Meadows School, Placerita Junior High, Hart High, and UCLA and has a master's degree from Loyola Marymount University. Eva is an amazing person who exceeds expectations in everything she does. As I write this book, she is a three-year cancer survivor who continues to fight that dreadful disease and advocates for the Metavivors that need research dollars to fight stage 4 metastasized breast cancer. She is married to Jon Crawford who works in the medical equipment industry. He has been a rock during the crisis, caring for his family and doing everything possible to keep everyone afloat. They have three wonderful kids 11-year-old Tucker, 9-year-old Hudson, and 7-year-old Layla. They live in Ventura.

Loring Air Force Base

I graduated from Bordentown Military Institute in June, 1960. I was not quite 17 years old and not very employable. I missed getting into West Point by the thinnest of margins and missed getting into Columbia University for financial reasons. Whatever money the family had; it had been spent on my military school education. I was pretty much on my own for college.

Because of that I felt the Air Force would give me the best chance of helping to pay for my education. So I enlisted. I entered basic training at Lackland Air Force Base in Texas, January 1961. In September I was assigned to Loring Air Force Base in Maine. I arrived on Labor Day to a balmy 75 degrees. It seemed like a great place in which to be stationed. The next day I was issued my gear. It consisted of thermal underwear, thermal socks, thermal boots, thermal sweater, thermal gloves, thermal mask and a thermal cap that could be rolled down over the ears. Lastly, I was issued a parka. It was not an indicator of warm, sunny days ahead.

Loring Air Force Base was a huge air force base in the northernmost part of Maine. It had about 40 B-52 bombers,

20 KC-135 tankers, and 25 fighter jets. Those fighter jets belonged to my unit, the 27th Fighter Interceptor Squadron. My squadron's mission was to patrol the northeast corridor of the Pinetree Line, the line between Canada and the U.S, and thwart any Russian bomber incursions. Mainly, it was defending against attempts to destroy the bomber force on the base. We took that mission very seriously.

The bombers held daily alerts. The alert alarms rang out throughout the base and all bomber crews rushed to their aircrafts. The ground beneath us would shake from the power of the revving engines of dozens of bombers and tankers. It was an incredible daily experience. I was told there was nothing to fear as the crews were just checking their aircraft systems. However, I was warned that if the aircrafts were being rushed to the runways, it meant real trouble. If the aircraft actually took off, it probably meant – nuclear war.

Whenever the bombers held alerts, our fighters would also alert. In the event of imminent attack, the bombers would go out first, followed by the tankers, and then by our fighters. One day in the late fall, on one of the coldest days I had ever experienced, the bombers held what I thought was one of their daily alerts. The aircraft noise was extreme as the ground shook extra hard that day. Our squadron of fighters alerted too. No big deal. It was a daily occurrence. Except this time the bombers began to rumble toward the runways. What the heck? All of a sudden the situation became extremely scary. "Jesus, Mary, Joseph," I prayed, "Let this not be what I think it is."

Bomber after bomber rolled onto the runways. Tankers queued behind them. Our fighters, not rolling yet, were at the ready. The sound was deafening. Then down the runway went the bombers. Louder, stronger, exhaust fumes almost blinding our eyes. Fast, then faster they streaked down the runways in pairs of twos. Our fighters started to roll next. My heart was pounding loudly in my chest!

Then, suddenly, the lead bombers pulled back on their throttles and didn't take off. The alert was over just like that. Everyone could breathe normally again. Not really. I couldn't breathe normally for days after that.

I wasn't certain what that was all about, but the scuttlebutt later was that a flock of birds heading south for the winter had tripped the radar systems causing the alert to take place. It was one of the scariest moments of my life.

In April of 1962, on yet another freezing night in northern Maine, I was on the flight line when a KC-135 tanker rolled onto the runway. Those tankers and their crews did great work. They performed mid-air refueling of the bombers. One mistake midair and both tanker and bomber go up in smoke. In my mind, you had to either be a super patriot or a crazy person to be part of a tanker crew.

The tanker revved its engines to a loud roar. The noise made me look in the tanker's direction. It started down the runway with its eight-man crew. Suddenly and without warning the tanker veered to the right and exploded in a ball of fire. I watched in horror as the tanker, full of jet fuel, was engulfed in flames. By the time the fire trucks arrived all eight crew members had burned to death. It was one of the saddest events I ever experienced.

United States Air Force Academy

In June, I entered the U.S. Air Force Academy in Colorado. Getting in was no easy task. To get in I had to be nominated by my congressman, pass a very tough physical, and get very high scores on my SAT's. Staying in great shape and studying every night was doable but getting my congressman to nominate me was another thing. Enter my sister, Linda.

Linda's best friend's mother worked for one of the political parties in New York City. On one of my visits to New York, Linda introduced me to her. We got along quite well. She asked me a lot of interview type questions. I answered them as honestly as I could and she promised she would mention me to my congressman. A couple of months later I got a letter from him telling me where to go for the physical and the academic testing required. I went, did very well and waited for his response. It came a couple of weeks later. I was nominated. The only thing left was for the Air Force Academy to give me an appointment. It came a month later and that June, I entered the academy.

I was blessed to be a United States Air Force Academy cadet. That was a great honor. I did very well there because of my previous military school experience. I was proud to have been in the Air Force Academy's top 5% of cadets in military leadership. That earned me a place on the Commandant's List.

While my time at Bordentown Military Institute helped me go from "inner city kid" to an "officer and a gentleman," my time at the Air Force Academy helped me go from citizen to patriot. How could it not? I got to meet and chat with some of the great men in American history. I met General Jimmy Doolittle, the man who led the very first air attack on Japan at the start of WWII. I met Colonel Victor Ferrari, who led a WWII bomber mission over enemy territory, was shot down, and escaped to safety using the allied underground network. Colonel Ferrari and I had a two-hour conversation one day when he taught me about values and why they were so important. I met Colonel Chuck Yeager at the Officer's Club at Oxnard Air Force Base in Oxnard, CA. He actually bought me a couple of beers. Chuck was the first person to break the sound barrier. And I met the great all American football player for Army, Heisman Trophy winner, Air Force Colonel Felix "Doc" Blanchard. He was 15 years removed from the gridiron, but he looked as if he could still carry the pigskin across any goal line. He was fit as a fiddle. How could

I not become a huge patriot after breathing the same air as those great men?

McGuire Air Force Base

I completed my Air Force career at McGuire Air Force Base in New Jersey. During that time, I married Patricia and she gave birth to Christine. We moved into a beautiful home not too far from base. I was assigned to the 539th Fighter Interceptor Squadron, another Air Defense squadron whose mission was to guard against Russian bombers coming in from the east.

McGuire Air Force base was pretty good duty for me and made my last year in the military a relatively easy one. Patricia and I got to know each other better while raising Christine. Weekends we usually traveled the 60 miles to visit relatives in New York City. During the week when I wasn't at the flight line, I was at the library or playing basketball. Nice duty.

Two things kept me from reenlisting. The first was that after seven years in the military I was ready for something else. The second was the Vietnam war. I had a young wife, an infant baby girl, and had already given years to the military. I just wasn't ready to go to war. The decision still haunts me a bit, but I decided not to re-enlist.

Overall, my Air Force career included flying back seat in the F-101 Voodoo fighter jet (once flying at twice the speed of sound), the T-33 trainer, and the T-29 flying school airplane. The majority of my college tuition was paid for by the Air Force and I spent four incredible years doing worthwhile things. Joining the Air Force was one of the best decisions I ever made.

CHAPTER FIVE

EAST COAST/WEST COAST

The Presentations Begin

The Mayor called the first candidate to the lectern for the first presentation. The candidate had everyone's attention. He was a longtime resident of Santa Clarita and truly a community leader. His presentation was solid and well delivered. He could be tough to beat.

As the procession of candidates began, my thoughts drifted to my late mother. Mami was a can-do woman. If she were there, she would have been whispering to me, "Don't worry, Willie. Everything is going to be all right. You're the one they're going to pick. I'm sure of it."

She probably would've spent the next few hours sitting by my side, holding my hand, and praying. My mother prayed every day of her life. As a little boy I remember her praying for our family, sometimes for patience, sometimes for money to pay the rent, and sometimes for food on the table. Every once in a while she would ask us kids to join her, on our knees, to pray extra fervently for something important.

God rewarded her with a good family and a good life, up until her last seven years. When she turned 80, she was diagnosed with a severe case of diabetes. Three years later she lost one leg to amputation. Three years after that she lost the other. One year after that she lost her life. During the last painful years, she never stopped praying and never lost faith. Whenever I visited her, she would beam with joy. She'd tell me how proud of me she was and ask me if I still prayed every day. God bless Mami's soul.

Mayor Smyth called more names. I tuned in and out of the presentations. Some candidates were outstanding while others were very good. All of them were willing to step up and compete for the seat. I always gave credit to people who were willing to step out of their comfort zones and try something new. It reminded me of my late father.

If he were there he would have said, "It's going to be a tough haul, son, but as I've always said, you have the ability to do anything you want to do. You can be anything you want to be. You just have to step out of your comfortable place and take some risks. I have faith in you. You'll see. Mami is right. You're the one they're going to pick."

My father's optimism did not come easy. He was raised in Puerto Rico during the midst of the depression when unemployment was at 40 percent. His family moved to New York City when he was a teenager. He was not happy to leave his beloved island of Puerto Rico. He rebelled. He refused to attend school in his new country and instead worked odd jobs mostly as a dishwasher and bus boy at local restaurants.

A year later and only 16-years-old, he falsified his age on the application and entered the Civilian Conservation Corps. The C.C.C. was a public works project focused on preserving the forests. The federal government created it for young Americans 18-years-old and over. My father worked for a year in the forests of Northern California. It was hard work and long hours, but he loved it. Hard work and long hours were never a problem for him.

After being drafted into the Army and serving three years in the war in the Pacific, Papi left the army with little education and training, and went back to dishwashing and bussing to feed his family. His greatest gifts were his inner drive and optimism. He drove himself to become a self-educated man who worked sometimes three jobs to give his family a chance to live better lives. And he never complained about it. He was optimistic that everything would be alright.

I remember the last time I saw him, which was at the end of his last trip to Santa Clarita. He was 90-years-old. We drove him to LAX to catch a plane back to New York where he lived with my sister Millie and her husband Bill. I got out of the car to help him with his baggage.

"What are you doing?" he asked. "Stay in the car before you get a ticket for illegal parking. I'm okay. I don't need any help."

I didn't listen and helped him get his baggage to curbside check in. Then I started to enter the terminal with him to help him get his wheelchair ride to his gate. "Hey, hey! I don't want you to take me any further. I'm not as old as you think. I can take care of myself. Now go back to your car and hope you don't find the police ticketing it."

I relented to his wishes, hugged, and kissed him, and smiled as we said our goodbyes. He smiled back, waved, and disappeared into the terminal. Two days later the phone rang in the middle of the night. It was my sister, Millie. My hero, my father, was gone. God bless Papi's soul.

University of Nebraska Omaha

In the fall of 1967, I was a senior at the University of Nebraska Omaha. My wife Patricia and daughter Chris had stayed in New York close to family. In Omaha, I was looking to rent a room and got a lead on a place on 33rd and Hamilton. It was a big house, three stories and a basement. Mrs. Spore and her husband Vincent owned it. They rented rooms to college kids. I met Mrs. Spore at the house. She offered me a glass of water and interviewed me as a potential tenant. She was a jovial lady. We got along very well and even laughed quite a bit together. Her husband was another story. During the interview, he returned home from work, metal lunch pail in tow. When he saw me he demanded to know who I was. Mrs. Spore told him I was about to be become their newest boarder.

He looked at me, looked back at her and declared, "He's colored. We ain't taking any colored kids here."

Mrs. Spore looked at him and laughed. She told him, "Why he ain't colored. He's Eyetalian!"

He looked at me with his sternest look and thought for a moment before saying, "Well okay. If he's Eyetalian."

I almost corrected them to say I was Puerto Rican, but I decided to leave well enough alone. I needed the room. Vincent Spore never got comfortable having me in the house, but Mrs. Spore and I became good friends. When I told her I was Puerto Rican, she wanted to know in what part of Italy that was.

International Club

I joined the campus International Club. We met weekly at lunch to share our experiences and to help one another through the trials of being "different" at the school. We had about 30 regular attendees at our meetings. Most of our members were of first generation European heritage from Ireland, England, Germany, Italy, Latvia, Poland and Romania. Some were from Latin America including a Cuban, a Colombian and myself. There were also members from the Philippines and Japan. That was my first real international encounter. We actually had real conversations about life in the different cultures. It was truly enlightening and rewarding for us all.

I became a casual acquaintance of Marlon Briscoe the great quarterback on the football team. Most people don't know that Marlon Briscoe was the very first black man to start at quarterback for an NFL team. He later went on to win two Super Bowl rings with the Miami Dolphins.

I spent time with wrestling coach Don Benning. Doctor Benning brought the first National Collegiate College Wrestling Championship to the state of Nebraska. He was the first black head coach of a predominantly white university. He's a member of the UNO Wrestling Hall of Fame and the Omaha Sports Hall of Fame. Once, I rode with him and his wrestling team in his automobile to a tournament at South Dakota University. His team not only won the tournament but won every single weight class championship. He was an incredible coach. More importantly, he was an incredible man.

Face-to-Face with George Wallace

In early 1968, Governor George Wallace of Alabama was considered one of the biggest racists in the country. It turned out he was speaking at the university and a good friend of mine and I had a class in the building where the racist was scheduled to speak. He was running for President of the United States under the American Party ticket. My friend Norma and I were not fans. Protesters were out by the hundreds in front of the building awaiting Governor Wallace's departure. When class let out, I said to Norma, "Look, George Wallace is getting ready to come out. I don't want any part of that. Let's go down the back stairwell."

She agreed and we took the back stairwell. When we reached the second floor, the door opened abruptly and out stepped two 6'6" plain clothes Alabama State Troopers. They slammed Norma into one wall and slammed me into another. Then all of a sudden, George Wallace appeared. Norma is white. He looked at her, and then slowly looked at me as his mouth formed an awkward smirk. Then down the stairwell and out the back door he went. He didn't want to go out the front door because of the protesters waiting for him. So he snuck out the back door and into a waiting limo. I literally came face-to-face with George Wallace in a stairwell, and the image is forever seared into my memory.

IBM

My senior year at Nebraska I sought after career opportunities post college. I interviewed with Ford, Standard Oil, and IBM. My goals were to get a job with good career training and to make money. In the mid-sixties, most college students dressed and looked nothing like the big corporations wanted. Except me. I had the insight to wear a white shirt, a plain blue tie and a navy blue blazer. Except for my brown skin, I was a campus recruiter's dream.

All three companies offered me a job. I chose IBM because it offered new technology and vast training opportunities. IBM offered to train me in business, marketing, and sales to the extent that it was akin to getting a master's degree in business.

I worked at IBM's Rego Park office in Queens, N.Y. I had one month of in-office training before I was sent to Newark, N.J. for six weeks of basic computer skills training.

Out of the 60 students in my class, I was the only person of color. There were people from all over the eastern half of the country including many southerners. We all had one mission in mind and that was to learn as much as we could so we could become successful IBM'ers. All 60 of us had been sent to the course by our branch managers with the order to be number one in the class. The competition was very intense. Welcome to IBM.

I didn't finish number one, or number two, or even number forty, but I learned a great deal about business and computers. And during the many evening discussions with classmates, I learned much about feelings on race across the country. Though some resisted, most of us were pro full integration and equal rights for all. It was a big step. "White" IBM was hiring people that were going to change it and make it even better.

My next training stop was Atlanta, Georgia where I received more computer training. I lived in an apartment with three other gentlemen. One was a black graduate of a black college. Another was an ex-army captain combat veteran who had spent two tours in Vietnam and drank too much. A third was an ex-marine captain whose experience in Vietnam was more in logistics than in combat. During class we all worked hard to be number one. But there could only be one. It wasn't me.

Outside of class we engaged in heavy discussions. Race, the Vietnam war, and career opportunities at IBM were key topics of discussion. Was IBM really opening itself up to being a place where everyone was welcome? Or were we just token hires? Were large corporations supporting a war that was killing our youth by the thousands each year? Or were they wanting the war to end? Our discussions included students from other rooms and soon we had to use a conference room because there were so many of us interested in having those discussions. We were just a bunch of recent college grads trying to express ourselves to one another and share our inner feelings out loud. It was so meaningful. Those discussions alone were as important to us as all the business and computer training we received.

It was the summer of '69. Atlanta then was not the Atlanta of today. Jim Crow was still alive and well. I remember walking into a barbershop for an overdue haircut.

I waited patiently for my turn. When it came, I was told someone was ahead of me. That was not the case, but I didn't argue and waited patiently. When my turn came up again, I stood up and walked to the barber chair and sat down before anyone else could cut in front of me. The barber looked surprised at my assertiveness. He told me he didn't think he could cut my hair. I asked why and he answered because he didn't know how to cut my type of hair. My type of hair? He didn't know how to cut wavy hair? I looked at him with my best "don't mess with me look" and told him to do his best because I wasn't going to leave the chair without a haircut. About half an hour later I walked out with a decent haircut, leaving the barber behind wondering why I didn't tip him.

In the little spare time that I had, I played recreational basketball at the nearby university, Georgia Tech. I loved playing basketball. It was great fun and excellent exercise until I broke my foot playing a pickup game one night. I spent most of the night in the hospital and was relegated to my apartment for almost a week before I could return to IBM. That morning I hobbled in on crutches and received a standing ovation as I entered the classroom. A standing ovation just for breaking my foot? No, not really. Word from New York was that one of my sales prospects had selected IBM as their vendor of choice and I was credited with a million dollar sale. That was the first of several million dollar sales I was to win in my career. IBM training laid the foundation for my sales success, and for that I am forever grateful.

MGM

In 1970, MGM Corporation was losing money hand over fist. Their movies were doing poorly and their music business was failing miserably. They decided to move their corporate headquarters from Manhattan to their studio in Culver City, California. As a part of that move, I was asked to help oversee the transition of their IBM computers to the new location. More than that, I was asked to move my family to California. Without hesitation I said yes.

Going from the conservative culture of IBM to the Hollywood culture of MGM was another culture shock for me. My dark pinstripe suits, white shirts, and conservative ties stood out like a sore thumb. My New Yorker fast talk, fast walk, and fast action was looked upon as "full of himself" stuff. In Hollywood culture, things are slower paced and more relation-centric. Big lunches, evening parties, and late night carousing was the norm. None of those were my thing so I didn't fit in. I tolerated working at MGM, but I didn't like it. It wasn't their fault. It was mine.

During my time at MGM, I met some big celebrities including David Janssen from the TV series The Fugitive and Bill Bixby, who starred in The Courtship of Eddie's Father. At MGM Records on Sunset Boulevard, I met the Osmonds, Lew Rawls, and Ritchie Havens, all popular singers of that time. I didn't meet Elvis Presley, but we passed each other several times at the studio and greeted each other in passing. One day he scared the bejesus out of me.

He was standing in front of the MGM Thalberg building surrounded by a bevy of beauties. I walked past them and up the front steps to the entrance door. A pretty lady standing by the entrance door pointed to Elvis and said, "He does that all the time. I'm standing here waiting for him and he's flirting with all those girls."

She leaned into me and gave me a peck on the lips. Nothing serious, just a peck. I was surprised, but hey, it was Hollywood. She smiled and stepped back. I smiled and walked into the building feeling strange, but good.

About 20 minutes later, I walked out of the building and headed toward my office. Elvis and the beauties were gone as was the kissing lady. Walking back to my office I noticed a large, black limousine creeping slowly behind me. I moved over a bit to let it pass, but the limo moved over too. Annoyed, I moved over closer to a wall. The limo almost brushed against me. By now I was really annoyed. Ready for a confrontation, I approached the limo just as the rear passenger window opened.

Sitting in the back seat, Elvis looked at me sternly and said, "I saw what you did with my gal." I thought I was about to get my head handed to me when suddenly he burst out laughing and said, "Oh, Man, I'm just kidding with you." Then he smiled, waved, and the limo drove away. Funny guy.

CHAPTER SIX

MY VIRGINIA

Brent Braun

Mayor Smyth continued to call names. It was interesting to try and figure out how each councilmember kept track of each candidate. They had to read the application, put a face to the candidate, and pay close attention to each presentation.

The Mayor called candidate number 12. It was Brent Braun. He was a retired federal law enforcement officer and had served as legal counsel to Galpin Motors. He was on the board of the Santa Clarita Valley Senior Center and had worked at a high level with other well-known charities. I didn't know him, but having read his application I considered him a real competitor for the appointment. Secretly, I hoped he would turn out to be extremely unbecoming and not well spoken. Instead, up walked a tall, fit, handsome man who spoke eloquently. When he was finished speaking, I knew he was going to be one of the finalists that night.

When the meeting began, I felt confident in my credentials and my ability to present well. I believed I was the leading candidate for the position. You don't go into a competition like that without feeling like you'll win. After watching and listening to Mr. Braun, I felt my chances drop to 50/50. But, instead of feeling down, I remembered what Mr. Borst at BMI told me, "If you want to be the best, you have to beat the best." I was determined to be the best.

Mayor Smyth called more names. And I thought of my lovely wife, Virginia.

Love at First Sight

I first saw Virginia while we were both working at MGM. I was walking out of the studio's east gate as she was walking in. She was the most beautiful woman I had ever seen. She wore a long, clingy dress that was bold and colorful. There was a bit of a sachet to her walk that was becoming and I could hear the clicking of her high heels on the pavement. Her hair was long, dark and wavy and parted down the middle. Her face was oval shaped with bright brown eyes highlighted by long eyelashes. She had a straight nose that belied ethnic background. Her cheeks were slightly prominent and her mouth, dressed in a beautiful smile, was sensuous and provocative. It wasn't just love at first sight. I was hit with the force of a lightning bolt.

I smiled at her as we passed and she smiled back at me. I couldn't resist another look and I turned around to look at her again. To my surprise and delight, she turned to look back at me. It only took ten seconds in passing but the sparks really flew. Then she vanished through the gate.

A couple of weeks later, I just happened to glance out of my office window and couldn't believe my eyes. There she was walking with a girlfriend toward a nearby coffee shop. I grabbed my jacket and sprinted after them. By the time I arrived at the coffee shop they were already seated. Smiling confidently, I approached their table and asked if they minded if I joined them. To my surprise, her friend abruptly replied, "Actually, yes we do."

Later for you lady, I wasn't about to be deterred. I pulled up a chair and sat down anyway. Ignoring her friend, I asked Virginia her name. I asked what she did at the studio. She said she was a legal secretary. I told her that surprised me. I thought she was an actress. She smiled and asked me what I did. I said I was a computer guy. She said that surprised her. She thought I was a movie producer or someone important since I wore a suit and tie. We both laughed at our mutual misassumptions. I asked how long she had worked at the studio. She said seven years.

"Seven years?" I asked incredulously. "How old are you?" I said louder than I intended.

Virginia looked around the coffee shop as my voice had attracted attention. She said she was 27. "Twenty-seven!" I shouted.

Admittedly, I was out of practice. She could have asked me to go away. Instead she smiled and asked me more about myself.

"I'm with the IBM systems group," I told her. "I transferred a year ago to Culver City from New York."

Virginia's friend was visibly annoyed, but neither of us cared. I asked Virginia for her phone number and she gave me her work extension. That was good enough for me. She gave me her million dollar smile as I got up to leave. I floated on a cloud back to my office.

Our First Date

It was a Wednesday, early afternoon, when I called Virginia to invite her to a party that a friend of mine at MGM was hosting that night. She was happy to hear from me. We engaged in some small talk before I invited her to the party.

"Oh, I'm sorry. I can't make it. I have a date tonight," she said.

Ouch. I was really out of practice. I tried to convince her to break her date but to no avail. The best I could get was a "maybe next time."

The party that night was a lot of fun, but I kept thinking about how much better it could've been if Virginia were there. The next morning I called her up.

"You missed a really good party," I told her.

She sighed into the phone and said, "I'm so sorry. What makes me feel worse is that my date stood me up."

"Stood you up? Who in their right mind would ever do that to a beautiful woman like you?"

I think I was starting to feel my groove. "I am going to make it up to you. I'm taking you out to dinner tonight," I said with complete confidence. She happily accepted my invitation. I was more than thrilled.

It was a busy day for me at the studio and that was good. It helped make the hours pass more quickly and kept me from becoming a nervous ball of energy. It also kept me from going to the bank to get cash. Why was that important? Because nobody used credit cards in those days and there were no ATM's. Every restaurant required cash. The problem was that I didn't realize I had no cash until it was too late. The banks were already closed and I was in my car on my way to take my dream gal to dinner. I had $2 in my wallet. Two lousy bucks.

New Yorkers are nothing if not resilient. I drove to a liquor store where I bought a half gallon bottle of Spanada wine. Look at it as a watered down version of "two buck Chuck." Cost: $1.98. So far so good. I had a bottle of wine and two cents in my pocket. Two cents wasn't going to pay for a meal so dinner out was no longer an option, but maybe dinner in was. I formulated a plan. I'd knock on her door and suggest a glass of wine before dinner. If we lingered long enough in conversation, surely she'd offer to cook. It could work.

When I arrived at Virginia's apartment, I took a deep breath and knocked on the door.

"Hello," she greeted me. "Just let me grab my shawl and I'll be right out."

"Hold on," I said. "I brought a bottle of wine for us to have a drink and maybe chat a bit before we go out."

She looked a little confused, but agreed and invited me in. "Go ahead and pour us two glasses of wine and put the rest of the bottle in the fridge, if you don't mind," she said. "I'll just clear a space on the coffee table for our glasses."

Oh, yeah, baby. The plan was working to perfection. Wine, conversation, some eats and who knows what else. I breathed a sigh of relief as I poured the wine. Then I opened the fridge and was caught off guard. The refrigerator was empty. I mean nothing. No food, no milk, no butter, not even a box of Arm & Hammer. What the heck? I pretended to look for more glasses and opened each of the cupboard doors. Nothing, nada, rien. How did she live? Didn't she eat? I needed a new plan and fast.

We drank more wine, made more small talk, and listened to a Cat Stevens album, Mona Bone Jakon.

"The restaurants close early on weeknights in this area," Virginia reminded me.

"I'm not hungry, if you're not hungry," I responded.

"I kind of am," she said.

Ignoring that and thinking fast, I poured each of us another glass of wine to buy more time. I restarted the album. "Would you like to dance?" I asked.

She said yes. We had danced through half the album when she emphatically announced she was completely starved. Curses, my plan was foiled. Just as I was about to confess to only having two cents in my pocket, there was a knock on the door. Virginia got up to answer it.

It was the guy who'd stood her up the night before. He started to apologize for having the wrong night, but she cut him short and said, "I have company."

He didn't take the news particularly well, and before storming off, thrust a large pizza and a 6-pack of beer into her hands, sputtering that she might as well enjoy it with her new friend. Ave Maria and praise the Lord. Pizza and beer!

New York, NY

I survived that night and got better at dating. I made sure I had money in my pocket, gas in my car, and a good plan for us to enjoy our evenings together. Over the next few months, listening and dancing to Cat Stevens as well as Roberta Flack albums, we fell in love.

One evening we had a special dinner together. The SS Princess Louise was docked at Terminal Island in L.A. At the time it was the largest floating restaurant in America. During that dinner we expressed our love for each other and began making plans for our future together.

Virginia had never been east of the Mississippi. She had never seen New York. She asked me a lot of questions about the city and my childhood. She was curious about my upbringing. I decided it was time she visit the Big Apple. I invited her to join me for a trip to New York City. Her answer caught me way off guard. "I'd love to," she said. "But I can't. My parents would never allow it." Say what?!

Wait a minute. A 27-year-old woman who has her own apartment and a good job can't take a vacation without approval from her parents? When I asked her why, she sheepishly replied that it was because I had been married before. She told me that her parents would never consider a divorced man for her. Her parents didn't even know I existed. Here I was sitting at third base in our relationship heading for home and Virginia was not even at bat yet. Virginia sensed my disappointment and concocted a scheme to accompany me to N.Y.C. without her parents knowing. A couple of weeks later we arrived in New York to take the Big Apple by storm.

First, we met up with my childhood friends Oscar Montalvo and Carlos Ramos along with Oscar's wife, Delia, and Carlos' fiancée, Ofelia. After a festive dinner at Benihana's in mid-town Manhattan, we met up for drinks in

Greenwich Village at the Cafe Wha. The next day was Sunday and Virginia and I still had a whole week to explore, adventure and enjoy each other's company. A visit to St. Patrick's Cathedral and Rockefeller Center was followed by a tour of Times Square. That evening we enjoyed a Broadway play, The Prisoner of Second Avenue starring Peter Falk, Lee Grant, and Vincent Gardenia. On Monday, we visited Battery Park in lower Manhattan and we caught a round trip ferry ride from there to Staten Island. Along the way we had a beautiful view of the Statue of Liberty. Later that day we went up to the top of the Empire State Building. It was a cold December evening especially at the top. No problem. Warm hugs and gentle kisses cure almost anything.

Tuesday we spent mostly in Central Park and along Fifth Avenue. We got to the northeastern part of the park and entered Spanish Harlem. Virginia had never seen anything like it. There was music everywhere, shops and bodegas every few feet, and more Puerto Ricans in one place than she knew even existed. Ave Maria Purisima! I introduced her to Puerto Rican soul food called cuchifritos. Not a good idea. I thought she was going to throw up. I didn't get it. I thought everybody loved hairy pig's ears and watery blood sausage.

We decided to go big or go home and took off on a two-day road trip to Washington, D.C. We visited the White House, the Washington Monument and the Lincoln Memorial. We were thrilled when California Senator, Alan Cranston, met with us and gave us gallery passes to the Senate chamber in the Capitol Building. We visited Arlington National Cemetery and the Tomb of the Unknown Soldier during a changing of the guard. Before we headed back to New York, we stopped for a wonderful meal in Georgetown. During that two day excursion we never felt rushed and still managed to do all that, including travel.

On Friday we visited the Guggenheim Museum. It was truly spectacular. After visits to the Museum of Natural History and the Museum of the City of New York, we were exhausted. We had a quiet dinner at our hotel and crashed till almost noon on Saturday. In the afternoon we went souvenir shopping for Virginia's family and friends.

Sunday morning we hit the airport and flew back to Los Angeles. We both had the most wonderful vacation we'd ever experienced. Virginia loved every minute of it. She had read about and seen pictures of New York City and Washington, D.C., but being there, she was overwhelmed by the magnificence of it all.

Meeting the Parents

I wish I could tell you that meeting her parents was a planned event, but it wasn't. I had moved into an apartment on Rochester Avenue about a block from Virginia's place on Carmelina Avenue. We spent most of our time at each other's apartments, but we hadn't made the jump to living together. One Sunday morning, Virginia and I took a walk together. She was wearing one of my shirts like a dress. Don't ask.

When we returned from our walk, there, waiting for us in front of my apartment building, were Virginia's parents. They'd spotted her car in front of the building and were waiting there for her. We were in deep pucky.

After berating us on the street, the Bidabes insisted on continuing the berating at their house not too far away on Granville Avenue. Reluctantly we agreed. I insisted Virginia change out of my shirt and into her dress before we went. It was the decent thing to do.

At the Bidabes we gathered around the kitchen table and took our punishment respectfully. Lilly cooked up a big Mexican meal, all the while continuing to berate us. Things finally seemed to be calming down when the food was served.

"Have some tortillas, Bill!" Lilly offered rather harshly. "And have some enchiladas too!"

I tried to figure out which were the enchiladas and which were the tortillas. There were so many plates on the table. Most contained food I didn't recognize. Puerto Rican food is not the same as Mexican food. The only Mexican dishes I knew of were chips, salsa, burritos, and margaritas. Apparently I lingered too long trying to decide and Lilly became agitated.

"So you don't like Mexican food, huh? And won't eat it? I don't understand it. What kind of food do your people eat?"

My people? This was not going well. I tried to make amends and ate as much as I could from almost every dish on the table. I say almost every dish because there was no way I was touching the menudo. Hairy pigs' ears are one thing but cow's stomach? No way.

Finally, everyone calmed down and the discussion became somewhat reasonable. Virginia told her parents that she loved me and I told them I loved her very much. We hadn't decided to marry yet but were headed in that direction. Her father, visibly upset at the fact that I was a divorced man with kids, strongly suggested that she go away to visit a friend in Oregon for a few months without seeing me. And when she returned, she could decide for herself whether she still felt the same about me.

I wasn't going to stand for that. Separation from Virginia was to me the dumbest thing in the world. I knew Virginia felt the same way. Oh, wait. She didn't. To my surprise and disappointment, Virginia agreed with her father. So, Virginia, now 28-years-old, was sent to Siberia, I mean Portland, Oregon, for a three-month hibernation from me.

I drove her to Portland in her car, and flew back to L.A. I couldn't believe that she'd actually left me. But she did. I came back to L.A. and I was alone. Being without Virginia was a weird experience. I had my own apartment and very few friends. I counted the days till she returned.

New York City and the Summer of '72

Three months later, in early June, Virginia returned to my loving arms. It had been a torturous separation but we'd survived it. Our love seemed stronger than ever. I thought she would move in with me, but she reminded me her parents would not stand for that. Instead, she found an apartment to share with a girlfriend and moved in.

We enjoyed each other's company to the fullest that June, but I was concerned. In my opinion she remained too close to her parents and went to great lengths to keep our paths from crossing. It appeared they were still struggling with the fact that I'd been married before. Virginia kept insisting that she loved me, but her behavior told me I was clearly second to her parents. The situation came to a head a few weeks later.

My employer was sending me on a three-month assignment to Wall Street. I remembered our first trip to New York and thought of the fun the two of us could have spending the summer there. But when I asked her, she declined.

"That doesn't make sense," I stammered. "Why won't you come with me?"

"I can't do that to my family, to my parents," she insisted.

Criminy! The parents issue again. I was incredibly offended and very frustrated. When it was time to go to New York, she took me to the airport and I abruptly said good-bye and boarded the plane. I wasn't happy and she knew it.

In New York my assignment was to attend a financial education course. Selling at the highest levels of large corporations required extensive financial knowledge and I didn't have that. This course was designed as a fast paced, full-time program that ended with the equivalent of a master's degree in finance. It was intense training that did not allow for much outside activity.

The good news was that I lived with two roommates from California in a mansion in Greenwich Village for three months. We got a steal on a summer rental. Our mansion had two stories, 2,000 sq. feet of living area on the first level that included two bedrooms, a living room, the kitchen and dining room. There was another 2,000 sq. feet of master bedroom upstairs. I got the master and thought it would've been great to have been able to share it all with Virginia.

It was wonderful living in Greenwich Village. However, I was still so upset and too proud to communicate with Virginia at all during my absence. When it came time to return to California, she dominated my mind. I finally picked up the phone and called her. She was really disappointed in my lack of outreach to her. We shared our feelings and agreed we would meet when I got back to California and go from there.

When I arrived in Los Angeles, Virginia and I met for dinner. It didn't take more than a few minutes before we both forgot the separation anger and continued on our love path toward marriage.

The fall of '72 was exciting. I was back with Virginia. We weren't living together, but we spent a lot of our time together. She got to know my young daughters, Christine and Lisa, and built solid relationships with them. Virginia is one of the most loving and caring people in the world. She really bonded well with them. Anytime she met with resistance, she was patient enough and smart enough to navigate her way through it. We had a wonderful time because we spent so much of it doing things together, absolutely bonding.

Marriage

In early 1973 Virginia and I decided to live together. Naturally, her parents were left in the dark. Later that year, I changed companies, got a good job at Xerox and felt very good about the future. It was time for us to marry. I knew it would make Virginia happy.

One night, alone in our apartment, I asked Virginia for her hand in marriage. Confident she would be overjoyed; I waited for her impassioned, "Yes!"

Nothing was ever easy in our relationship. Her exact words were, "We'll see. You need to talk to my father."

Oh, boy.

She made me wait a few days before I talked to her dad. Thank goodness he'd finally realized that, even though I was a divorced man with children, I was a good man and a good match for his daughter. Her parents blessed the union and we were married on January 27, 1974. It was the best move I ever made.

CHAPTER SEVEN

XEROX

Ana Isela Dwork

Mayor Cameron Smyth called the 24th speaker. She was Ana Isela Dwork. She stepped up to the microphone and said she was born in Cuba. Her family escaped the Castro regime. When they arrived in the United States they had no resources and were unable to speak English. Through hard work, dedication, determination, and education they succeeded. Ana earned a bachelor's degree from California State University Northridge, a master's degree in administration, and a doctoral degree with a specialization in autism. She had raised three children, now all successful professionals, and was a grandmother of three. She taught at Canyon High School and was an assistant principal at La Mesa Junior High. She said she had done extensive work volunteering in the community and was a small business owner and real estate investor.

Ana was very professional in her presentation. She spoke clearly, slowly, and eloquently. I was concerned with her good qualifications as well as the facts she was a successful product of the American Dream and she was a Latina woman. Those qualifications could be fatal to my chances. I felt my odds drop from 50/50 to 30/70. Brent and Ana were definitely in the game.

The Mayor called three more names. I tried to listen to every word, but again my mind wandered. This time to my days at Xerox Computer Services.

John Wooden

As a manager at Xerox Computer Services, I was given the responsibility of orchestrating our annual kickoff meeting. It was an event that brought our division's key managers together for motivation and inspiration to work hard to meet our goals in the new year. As our guest speaker for the event, I chose to ask the recently retired great U.C.L.A. basketball coach, John Wooden. Choosing him was one thing. Getting him to agree was something else.

Our event team met to discuss it. We were willing to pay up to $3,000, a hefty sum in those days, for his appearance. We had the entire infrastructure for the event in place. All John Wooden needed to do was show up, have lunch and speak for about an hour. Easy peasy. I was ready to call his agent. I called U.C.L.A. to get his agent's name and was told Mr. Wooden didn't have an agent and handled requests to speak personally. To my surprise, not only did they give me his home phone number, but he himself answered when I called.

"Hello Mr. Wooden. My name is Bill Miranda. I am a manager at Xerox. We have a sales kickoff meeting on Thursday, January 29th and we would be honored to have you as our guest speaker. It's a lunch meeting," I blurted, hoping my nervousness talking to the legend would not be obvious in my voice.

"Thank you very much, Mr. Miranda, that's very kind of you," John said. "I would be honored to do that but unfortunately that day doesn't work for me. Perhaps another time."

I've made good decisions in my career and a lot of dumb ones, but this one took the cake. I didn't listen and instead tried to pressure him into changing his mind. "Mr. Wooden," I pressed. "We are bringing in dozens of key executives from all over the country for this event. Is it possible that you could change your previous commitment to attend our event?" I asked.

"No Mr. Miranda. Thursdays I'm not available at all. That's my babysitting day. I'm sorry." His voice was gentle and kind.

I pressed harder. "Mr. Wooden, couldn't you find another babysitter for that day?"

"Mr. Miranda," his voice got a bit stern. "I have a commitment to babysit on Thursdays and I keep my commitments. Surely a man in your position understands that."

I had crossed the line. With my tail between my legs I answered meekly, "Yes, sir. I understand. I'm so sorry. I didn't mean to ask that." And with that we politely said our goodbyes.

That afternoon I met with the event staff and told them what had transpired. They were incredulous. First off, they couldn't believe I spoke directly with John Wooden. More importantly, they couldn't believe how badly I'd botched the call. The event staff pushed me to change the date of the event to whenever he was available. I argued that everything for the event predicated on it being held on that date.

"Change the date," they insisted.

I said, "Why would we do that?"

"Because it's John Wooden!" was their unanimous reply.

So I called Mr. Wooden again. He was very gracious with me considering I acted like a jerk before. I asked him when he'd be available to us and we agreed upon Friday, January 30, one day later than our original date.

"We can pay $3,000," I told him.

"My fee is $500 and that will be enough," he answered.

We hung up the phones very cordially and I jumped as high as I could with joy. I had gotten John Wooden for our kickoff meeting. When I told the team at Xerox they were ecstatic. John Wooden was an exceptional draw. Enrollment for the event almost doubled. As the date approached we had to turn people away for lack of space to put them.

On the day of the meeting, Mr. Wooden arrived early. We sat at a table together and had a wonderful conversation about family and commitment. After lunch he got up and presented his famous, Pyramid of Success. I marveled at how well he presented and how really centered that man was. Being with John Wooden was one of the highlights of my life.

Married with Three Children

While things were hopping at work, life at home was also hectic. Virginia and I spent the first two years of marriage still getting to know each other better. We bought our first home, a small 2-bedroom, 2-bath house in West L.A. But it wouldn't be long before we decided we needed a bigger house. With my two girls visiting regularly and

Virginia becoming pregnant in early '76, we were on the grow. We bought a big house in Ladera Heights. It had three bedrooms, two baths, a family room, living room, big kitchen and a swimming pool. We were doing well and had become a party of five.

One evening Virginia and I held a party for the local Xerox management team. The managers came with their partners. Everyone loved our house that Virginia had decorated beautifully. One of the managers approached me that evening saying he couldn't believe I could afford such a nice house. Jokingly, he asked me if I was selling drugs. Insult aside, I reminded him that I was one of the company's leading salesmen and my wife worked as a legal secretary in the entertainment industry. Yes, we could afford the house and, no, we did not sell drugs. I guess he thought Latinos couldn't afford nice homes without doing things outside of the law.

The Passovers

I had five good years at Xerox. I joined as a salesperson, became a manager, and received excellent

111

management training. My time there was enlightening, productive, and enjoyable.

My problem with Xerox was that I was being passed over for promotions for which I felt I was more than qualified. At first I thought maybe they didn't think I was ready. I felt ready, but maybe they didn't think I was. I tried hard to promote myself.

I applied for a branch manager opening in Atlanta, Georgia, and was told no. "Atlanta's not a good environment for you," they said. What they really meant to say was, "We're not going to have a Latino be the branch manager in Atlanta." Shortly after that, there was an opening in Washington, D.C. "Well, Washington, D.C., that's government and you have to deal with a lot of different bureaucracies. We're not sure that's for you either." When I questioned them about it, they replied, "Well, we are wanting the right fit for you." Then came another opening, this one in Boston. I received another tiresome excuse. Then came San Francisco. And yet another excuse. Then came a San Diego opening.

I'm a Latino. If I can't be a branch manager in San Diego, then I can't be a branch manager anywhere. Sorry, they passed me up yet a fifth time. I had had enough. I turned in my resignation. The writing was clearly on the wall. Bill Miranda ain't getting a branch at Xerox. Even the hairs on the back of my neck stood up with my anger at being passed over. I had all my ducks in a row. I knew the president. I knew all the people involved. I knew the whole management chain. I was good at what I was doing and I was still being passed over. I was pissed and turned in my resignation.

Within an hour of resigning, the president of our division called me into his office.

"Bill," he said. "You're not leaving Xerox. When this meeting is over, I guarantee you will still be with Xerox." He told me I was one of the most valuable people in the company.

"We need to keep you, Bill. Xerox needs you."

"If Xerox needs me, why in the hell was I passed over five times for a branch manager's job," I fired back.

"The first time I wasn't too upset. The second maybe a little. The third pissed me off and the fourth time really pissed me off. The fifth time you got my resignation. You tell me. What should I have done? When you're telling me Xerox needs me and people like me, and you're running me out by not promoting me, what am I supposed to do?"

He promised the next promotion would be mine. But it was too late. Damage done. We shook hands, wished each other luck, and I walked away from Xerox. I wasn't going to be passed up one more time for a job that I was more than qualified to have. If there had been an issue with my performance or my character, Xerox had the responsibility to bring it to my attention for correction. Those things should have been on my evaluation, but they weren't. They weren't there because my job performance and character were evaluated as above average to outstanding in every single category. So why was I passed over so many times? I think I know. I didn't fit their mold.

Virginia Quits Her Job

About the same time I was having issues with Xerox, Virginia had an issue with her legal secretarial job. Her employer, one of the major movie studios, wanted to do more for their affirmative action program by creating a position in the human relations department for a Latina woman. She applied knowing this would be a promotion. She was interviewed and was told she had the job. She was happy when she told me that evening and wondered how soon before she would start.

A couple of weeks later, she went to work only to find out there was a change. The new position was put on hold and she in fact didn't have it. Virginia's boss, who did not support Virginia's leaving for a better position, had been giving her a hard time to the point where during a conversation she told Virginia, "You can't help it if your father was a wetback."

Virginia had had enough and stormed out of the office. Her fellow office workers overheard the discussion and were shocked by it. Virginia walked outdoors for over an hour to cool off. She was as angry as she could be. She'd made up her mind. She was quitting immediately. She stormed back into her office, gathered her things, and waved goodbye to her fellow office workers. They gave her a standing ovation as she left.

Virginia had no problem getting another job. She was very talented and dedicated to her work. In fact, her new job came with better pay, less stress and more benefits. I didn't have a problem finding work either. My new job paid a lot more and offered incredible new challenges. When one door slams shut, another one opens. My door opened eventually to Paris.

CHAPTER EIGHT

PARIS!

Halfway Through

The Mayor announced the names of the next three speakers. We were halfway there. To their credit, the councilmembers listened and watched intently. The review process had to be arduous for them. Each councilmember had to review each of the 51 applications thoroughly. Who was the candidate? Why did they apply? How did they qualify? Who were their references?

Some of the candidates wanted one-on-one meetings with councilmembers. None were refused to my knowledge. It had to be a grueling experience for the councilmembers. Sitting there listening to presentations, one after another, knowing that the decision they were about to make that night would be vital to shaping the council for the future. No doubt it was a heavy burden weighing on each one of them.

The City Manager, Ken Striplin, sat nearby. Although he was not a decision maker in this case, he had to know the selection would affect his job and those of the city staff. Having been with the city for many years, he had experience working with many councilmembers. Some had been easy to work with in my opinion and others, not so much. It's best when the city council and the city staff work together to serve the needs of the citizens. I wondered if he had a favorite.

The Mayor called three more speakers. I listened a bit here and there, but just couldn't concentrate. I thought about our adventures in gay Paree.

Data General Corporation

When I joined the Data General Corporation, a Massachusetts based Fortune 500 minicomputer manufacturer, I felt like I went from the perfectly structured Xerox to what was more akin to the wild west. Their mantra was, "If you're making money for us, we love you. If you're not making money for us, we're kicking you out the door."

I joined as a major accounts salesperson whose first assignment was to "save" a major account that had already been lost to IBM. It seemed to everyone to be an impossible mission. In the spirit of the wild west, I decided to win it back. It was an international patient care company with facilities throughout the U.S. The problem was how to share computer data with all their facilities.

IBM's solution was called central processing using mainframes. Store all the data in one place, a large mainframe computer, and share it where needed to computer terminals via phone lines. It was like having big Mack trucks loaded with goods sent to deliver packages all over the country. Very slow, very inefficient and very costly.

Data General sold much smaller minicomputers. For those who are unfamiliar, a minicomputer is like having a van. Big Mack's purpose is to transport large loads for long distances. The vans have their purpose too, hauling smaller loads shorter distances. Mainframes handled huge databases but were slower to respond. Minicomputers handled much smaller databases but were much quicker to respond. Large medical companies needed both, but when I took over the account, the patient care company was not convinced. My job was to convince them.

I partnered with a young woman who was extremely creative and knew technology inside and out. I didn't know the technology nearly as well, but I knew the selling process and how to deal with the decision makers involved. Working closely together over several months, techie lady and I put together a presentation for the executives of the patient care company that knocked their socks off. The gist of our presentation was this: "You've got hospitals all over the country that need the data. They can't wait for the Mack truck. They can't wait for the mainframe to deliver the data. We have vans that can go and deliver the data very quickly, and the vans are minicomputers. We are proposing the future: distributed computer processing."

Distributed computing processing was the idea of housing local data on local minicomputers and company wide data on regional mainframes. That created the best of both worlds for the company. They loved the concept, especially after we demonstrated how it worked. We landed a multi-million dollar contract from that sale. I went from just another gunslinger to being Wyatt Earp overnight. I was viewed as the guy who cleaned up the mess and brought prosperity to the commercial side of Data General.

Because of that success, I was promoted to the corporate office in the Boston area, Westboro, Massachusetts. Just after New Year's Day, 1981, my family moved from the beautiful Los Angeles weather to the brutal winter of '81, Boston.

The Boston area was magnificent for its historical value and high-energy community. It was less than magnificent in one area, weather. Weather, sometimes barely bearable, made me laugh and cry at the same time. I remember one especially cold and snowy afternoon driving past a gas station when I saw a friend of mine visiting from Los Angeles trying to gas up his car. He didn't have any cold weather clothes and didn't know how to use the pump. It was hilarious watching him fighting the wind and cold while trying to figure out how to use the gas pump. But then I, in full cold weather regalia, got out of my car to help him. I told him to get into his car and that I would gas him up. I did and sent him on his way. Then I got back to my car almost crying from the cold.

We couldn't wait for the spring and the good weather. Well, not so fast Pilgrim. Have you ever heard of the Gypsy Moths? Those invading insects ate everything in sight! Flowers? Gone. Bushes? Gone. Trees? Naked. One night we got home from an outing and found them on our front door by the thousands. By the thousands!

Overall our stay in the Boston area was very rewarding. We very much enjoyed our one-year stay. We visited historic sites, great college campuses and took beautiful scenic drives all summer long. When fall and winter arrived we went into hibernation just like most sane people did. Come Christmastime, it was time to move on again.

Paris Part One

I was a middle manager in Westboro awaiting promotion into the executive ranks when an opening occurred in Data General Europe headquartered in Paris, France. There were some pretty tough requirements for the job including two potential game breakers. First, you were required to have an engineering degree. The company wasn't going to spend that kind of money to move someone overseas who was unable to master the technology of the future. Check. I had that one. The other was the ability to speak three languages. The office language was English, the language of France was French so that's why both English and French were required. The third language was required because we dealt with so many countries that we needed many different languages in our Paris office in order to do business. I spoke English and Spanish fluently. I'd learned French in high school and from numerous excursions into Quebec, Canada during my Loring Air Force Base days. So, thankfully, I met the requirements for the position.

Having met all the requirements and being excited to go live in Paris, our family spent the month of December preparing for the move. It wasn't easy telling Lisa and Eva that we were moving again, especially when it was to another country. It took awhile for them to get used to the idea. Virginia and I had a December we'd rather forget.

It was yet another Christmas season we could not fully enjoy. Not only did we have to do all the usual things that moving entails, but we had a very major time and emotional disruptor: French lessons. Yes, both Virginia and I had to attend full immersion Berlitz language lessons. Full immersion meant one-on-one classes for eight hours a day for four weeks. Let me set the stage for you.

It's Christmas season in New England. Hibernators are braving the weather to join the Christmas spirit, shop till they drop, drink till they stink and otherwise enjoy themselves. Not us. Not Virginia and not me. If ever there was a recipe for divorce this was it. Anytime a family has to move there is family stress. Every Christmastime there is family stress. And taking language immersion classes on top of that? Put them all together into one neat package and get ready to call the divorce attorneys.

Actually, I thought our first week of language training went well. Think of our instructors as good cop and bad cop. I had good cop. He was a young handsome Moroccan man who was kind and gentle and worked nicely with me when I struggled a bit with the language. Virginia had bad cop. She was a "maleficent" type before there was Maleficent. I could hear her from time to time yelling at Virginia, "Fait attention!"

At the start of the second week I took one for the team. I was intent on saving my marriage. I offered to switch instructors. Virginia agreed not to bash my head in if we did. It was a fair trade. For the rest of language training Virginia was very happy with Mr. Morocco and I was in purgatory with Maleficent. Marriage saved.

Once we got past all the drama, Virginia and the girls, Lisa and Eva, (Christine was a senior in high school in Cincinnati and couldn't go with us), were very excited about the move to Paris. Virginia loved art and loved to paint. Paris was considered by most the capital of the arts.

In early January, 1982 we arrived in Paris. The first two weeks, we stayed in a hotel near the Eiffel Tower. Virginia arranged for the girls to attend the American School of Paris about 20 miles by bus from our new home. We moved to the western part of metropolitan Paris in what was called the Anglo American suburbs. We had a beautiful two story house about 50 yards from the Seine River. There were three neighboring houses to our right: two French couples and a German/French couple. In the three houses to our left lived Irish, English, and Irish/English couples. If you're keeping score, that's five French, two English, two American, one German and one Irish on one street.

My world was simple. Get up in the morning. Take a long bath while I read the international papers, kiss the family goodbye, and take the awful RER train to La Defense where I worked. Every third week, I would travel outside of France to visit one of our offices in Frankfurt, Zurich, Amsterdam, Stockholm, London and Warrington, a city in the northern part of England.

When I left Westboro, I was entitled to two weeks' vacation. In Paris I was entitled to four weeks' vacation. And since I had over two years with the company, I had six weeks total. Wait, there's more. Since I was over 35 years old they added two more weeks for 8 weeks total vacation time. Europeans work to live. They don't live to work like many Americans.

My very first day, I arrived at work an hour early. I needed a security guard to let me in. Nobody walked into the office until 9:00 a.m. and it was barely 8:00 a.m. The executives came in around 9:30 a.m., and my boss came in at 10:00 a.m.

Bewildered, he came into my office and asked, "Why did you come in so early?" He was serious. He told me managers didn't get in until 9:30 and executives closer to 10:00. That way no one gets seen if they are a few minutes late. Welcome to France.

The workday ended at 5:00 p.m. I wasn't quite finished with what I was doing so I continued working in my office.

My boss walked in again and asked, "What are you doing?"

"I still have a few things to complete and I will leave in about half an hour," I responded.

"No, no, no," he said. "Your job is to be with the employees. They are downstairs at the bar."

What a country.

Virginia's world was quite chaotic until she became accustomed to the European lifestyle. Initially, she had to deal with the kids, furniture shipments and arrivals, purchasing a car, and even learning how to shop for groceries in a foreign country. Once she'd settled in, she got up early, got the kids to the school bus, made breakfast and kissed me goodbye. Then, after a few minutes of putting the house in order and getting herself ready, she was off to tea and crumpets with her international companions. What a life.

However, there were some hiccups along the way. The first was mine. After a few short weeks I couldn't stand riding the RER anymore. Virginia told me to suck it up and fight through it. I whined like a two-year-old and insisted on getting a second car. We did. A 1976 Honda Accord. Point aside, there were about 30 of those cars in all of Paris. I was very happy. One day I got home and Virginia greeted me with a frown. It turns out the neighbors were questioning why we ugly Americans had to have two cars. No other family had two. I didn't care. There was no way I was giving up my Honda.

Ironically, three weeks later, circumstances forced me to give up my Honda for over a month. Circumstances meaning Virginia. She'd crashed her Renault station wagon into the American School of Paris school bus while our girls were waiting to board. Don't ask. I wasn't there. I got three versions of the same story and none of them matched. The

Renault was almost totaled and it was going to take over a month to get fixed. Back to that miserable RER train I went.

The first three months living in Paris were a period of adaptation for us. The next three months were a period of excitement. Paris television only had two channels. They actually had three, but two of them showed the exact same programming at the exact same time. Usually television had nothing good so we just turned it off. Ten minutes of French radio gave us all headaches so we turned that off too. There was no internet in that era and no DVDs. There was, however, the game of Clue. We played Clue almost every evening and bonded very well as a family.

We took day trips into Paris on weekends. The Champs-Élysées was our favorite destination. From there we could visit the Arc de Triumph, Place de la Concorde, the Louvre, the Jardins des Tuileries, or just people-watch at one of dozens of cafes along the street. Sometimes we changed our routine and visited the Île de la Cité to see Notre Dame Cathedral and the vendors along the Seine River. Other times we chose to walk across the Pont Alexandre III, one of the most beautiful bridges in Paris, to Les Invalides to visit

Napoleon's tomb. Often we walked along the river to the Jeu de Paume to view the great paintings of the impressionists.

In early April 1982, I was invited by a Member of Parliament to attend a meeting at Parliament House in London. It was a meeting of high-tech professionals including guest speaker, Gene Amdahl, the father of the IBM 360 family of mainframe computers. When I told Virginia I was going to London, she asked if she and the girls could go, too. I said of course and I drove us there in our Honda. When we got to the English Channel at Calais, car and family boarded a hovercraft, an amphibious airplane, that transported us across the channel. It was quite an adventure. Another was disembarking in Dover and driving my left-hand-drive car on the left side of the roads. It was crazy confusing. I had to concentrate so hard I got a headache. My gals were scared and laughing hysterically as I barely missed hitting other cars and objects by a hair. Everyone, especially me, was happy when we arrived safely at our hotel. We had a lovely evening and the next morning I was off to Parliament House.

Prior to our arrival in London, there had been unrest off the coast of Argentina which involved a territory of the United Kingdom, the Falkland Islands. It was becoming obvious that a war could break out at any time. When I arrived at Parliament House, the minister greeted me warmly. Five security check points later (thank you IRA), we entered a wonderful hall with lots of statues and paintings of prominent people in British history.

I noticed a statue of Lord Falkland and stopped a moment, commenting to the minister, "I hope you don't have to go to war because of the tension in the Falkland Islands."

"Well, at least nothing's going to happen today," he replied.

I looked at my watch and did a quick calculation. We're in the U.K., Falklands are in another much earlier time zone. "Invasions usually take place in the morning," I said. "It's not morning yet over there."

In the meeting room there was a video screen periodically flashing different numbers. I asked what the numbers meant and was told it was a paging system. Each minister had a personal number. The minister asked us to try to ignore the screen unless all the numbers scrolled up at one time. If they did, it meant all the ministers were wanted immediately in chambers. In other words it meant there was an emergency. To my horror, a short time later all the numbers started flashing. The minister turned pale and rushed out.

He returned 20 minutes later, walked over to me and said, "You were right. The Argentines just invaded the Falklands."

The next two months we were glued to BBC radio. The reporting was riveting. First the outrage over the attack. Then the resolve to fight back and the formation of the fleet to go almost halfway around the world to retake the islands. And, as the fleet sailed to the Falklands, the daily reports continued as the ships prepared to go to war. It was like listening to a soap opera only it was real.

Over the next few months, the British retook the Falklands and won the war. The brutal Argentine junta was totally defeated politically when it showed it could not win a war against a country that had to travel halfway around the world to fight. In Britain, the end of the short war was a time of celebration and a reminder of Britain's days of glory.

Bill in Paris

At Buckingham Palace

The Gals at Versailles

Happy Couple in Montesson

Paris Part Deux

I was a runner most of my adult life. Running was a way to stay in shape both physically and mentally. I ran five to ten miles almost every day, rain or shine, home or away.

Running hadn't caught on in Montesson in 1982. When I ran early each morning, the shopkeepers, getting their shops ready to open, would laugh and jeer at me. "Vous etes un américain fou!" You are a crazy American.

By the end of the summer the shopkeepers were super friendly, "Bonjour Monsieur!" they shouted to me with smiles on their faces. That's the French. Until they know you they appear not to like you. Once they know you they consider you a good friend.

By the time the summer rolled around, we were ready for a vacation. Stop! I almost flinched as I wrote that. Imagine, living the lives we were living while in Paris then writing that we needed a vacation. Really?

We chose the Mediterranean coastal resort of L'Escala in the Costa Brava part of Spain. My parents joined us from New York. We drove the Renault from Paris to our resort. The first week was incredibly beautiful and restful. Virginia and I enjoyed our walks along the beach and the solemnity of it all. We enjoyed the second week, too, but for different reasons. On July 1st, L'Escala exploded in population from several hundred people to over 10,000. The World Cup of

Football (soccer) was held in Spain that year. No more solemnity. Now it was all about drinking, dancing, and partying. It was a great change of pace for us. We loved it.

Later that summer we took a trip to Normandy to visit the site of the 1944 World War II invasion. We visited the museum in Arromanches and the American Cemetery in Colleville. It made us prouder than we already were to be Americans.

That summer I took a two-week business trip to Sweden. I loved running in the beautiful hills outside of Stockholm. As Swedes were runners, I encountered many of them on my morning runs. What a beautiful country and a beautiful people who truly enjoy life.

By the end of summer the four of us had become Europeans. Lisa and Eva learned European history and culture at school. Their friends included many international students. Lisa played basketball for the school. Her away games were held in Norway, Italy, Switzerland and other countries in Europe. I helped her board the famous Orient Express one night, and when she returned I asked how she enjoyed that historic train across the Alps. She told me she didn't see anything. She slept the entire trip. Kids.

Virginia became the most European of the family. She enjoyed everything about Paris. She loved the beauty of it all, the architecture, the gardens. She loved both the fast pace in the city and the slower pace outside of it. She took it all in. Mostly she liked the people we got to know. Every day was an adventure for her.

Virginia is an artist. She paints mostly in oils. Paris was an ideal place to study painting and improve her skills. With my encouragement, Virginia contacted an art teacher in Paris and signed up for instruction. Once a week, Virginia "donned her beret", carried her art supplies and drove to the RER station where she took the train into Paris. There she changed to the Metro, and then again to another line, finally arriving at her destination. From there she'd walk several blocks to the building and hike five flights of stairs up to the studio. It paid off. Her artistic sensibilities blossomed and the joy she received from it was worth the effort.

I started the Paris adventure as the closest one of us to being European, and I ended up as the least European of all. Sure, I was part of the multicultural community both at work and at home, but inside myself I was as American as apple pie. When people discovered I was an American, most would smile widely and ask me about America. When I told them I was from California they almost swooned. Some had visited America and loved it. Those that hadn't hoped someday they could. I was so proud to be an American, and I was beginning to miss home. The company offered me a new position back in L.A. and I jumped on it. And for the third year in a row at Christmas time, we prepared to move to a new home.

CHAPTER NINE

ARTWORKS

Back at the Council Chambers

Mayor Smyth announced the next speaker. It was a businessman well known in our community. I listened to him and thought his presentation was good and very well delivered. He quoted Martin Luther King (always a good thing) and went on to say that, if selected, he was ready to serve. He said he was a team player and not afraid of hard work. He mentioned that the night's efforts would affect his family's lives and that he wanted to be a part of building the legacy we pass on to future generations.

The timer went off cutting him short, just a bit. The businessman was a known leader in our community and well liked. He too had the potential to win. We still had about a dozen and a half speakers to go. The councilmembers continued to listen intently to each speaker, but I couldn't stop thinking about Virginia's passion for art and how it blossomed into something big.

Mourning Armand

When Virginia's father passed away, she didn't have time to mourn. She threw herself into moving her mother Lilly to Valencia, adapting to her new home, and reuniting with our family. It took the rest of 1983, and a good part of 1984, until she accomplished all she needed to do. It was time for her to mourn.

I reminded her that her art instructor in Paris had encouraged her to continue pursuing her art when she returned home. I remembered how happy she was taking instruction at the Paris studio, honing her skills under her instructor's watchful eye. So I suggested she take art classes. She seemed enthused by the idea and signed up for classes under master artist, Larry Gluck, at the Mission Renaissance Art Studio in L.A. Her passion for art returned and her true healing took place.

Going into Teaching

While in her second year as a student, Larry approached Virginia and asked if she'd like to help teach classes. Teaching was the last thing on her mind. Virginia was never comfortable being the center of attention. She preferred anonymity. But with my encouragement she decided to give it a try. Larry told her that her work was outstanding and her demeanor was right for teaching. He was kind and gentle and never full of himself. He was about helping others be the best artists they could be.

Larry had a large number of children in his art school and needed more instructors. He was thrilled when Virginia agreed to assist with the kids. Thus, Virginia became an art instructor with a focus on teaching kids the basics of art, as taught by the masters of art.

First came drawing. If you don't draw well don't expect to paint well. Students had to learn to draw before they moved on to the next stage. Mostly, they drew still life. Once students gained competence in drawing they were introduced to charcoal for shading, and pastels for color. Not until the kids showed competence at each level could they move on to the next. Children are impatient by nature. Some walked into the class paintbrushes at the ready. Virginia would call upon her motherly instincts to kindly, yet firmly, inform them there would be no painting until they completed each of the earlier stages.

Larry mentored Virginia well. He taught her the finer points of painting and giving instruction. Virginia valued the skills she was acquiring and developed into quite an artist and an excellent instructor. Her confidence level rose and she was happy. Although she would never get over the loss of her father, she was now in a good place knowing he would be very proud of her.

After a year of teaching for Mission Renaissance, Larry approached her with another offer. He offered Virginia the opportunity to start her own art school in Valencia. He provided the framework of the business as well as being her adviser. Virginia was to pay him a royalty fee for his services. After discussing it with me, she accepted. That was the beginning of Artworks Studio & Gallery.

Artworks Studio & Gallery

The first year of the studio was a bit of discovery. Virginia had Larry's guidance, but basically it was her show. Should she teach adults, or children, or both? Should the studio offer space for five, ten, or even more students? Never having run her own business before, she didn't know what to expect or how to plan properly. Being steeped in the business world, I tried to help as much as I could. Sometimes she accepted my advice and other times she followed her own instincts.

By the second year, Virginia had the studio she needed. It was located in the Plaza Posada on Lyons Avenue. She could comfortably teach eight students at a time. Her focus was on teaching children. The kids loved her and so did their parents. The art instruction was excellent, and more importantly, she cared about every single child. It wasn't long before she outgrew the studio and had to move to a much larger space.

Over the next ten years the studio grew to ten classes per week, averaging 12 students per class. Virginia did most of the teaching, but also hired teaching assistants. I marveled at how well she did. She was a small business owner who was doing well financially, while providing a much needed service to her community.

Art is a way to express oneself and many of Virginia's students needed to be there. It was more than art class. It was a haven where each child could express themselves in their own way. Through the years Virginia received many personal letters, notes, and cards from students thanking her for changing their lives. Many brought her to tears. She had no idea of the impact she had on the kids and their families. It was truly a blessing for her.

Artworks at Home

In 2001, we decided we needed to downsize the studio. The rent kept rising and Virginia was ready to slow down just a little. We converted our back patio into a small studio that could fit nine students comfortably.

The studio continued to flourish. Fewer students meant fewer revenues, but no rent meant more profits. It worked out just fine. Artworks was never intended to be a big money venture. It was intended to promote art and give others a place to develop their talents. Artworks succeeded in both of those goals.

Virginia wanted to offer a Friday morning class for adults, but she was doubtful it would generate much interest. To her pleasant surprise the class filled up quickly. There was 85-year-old "Mr. D" and six ladies. He playfully called them his harem. The art produced by them was very, very good thanks to Virginia's instruction, and their passion, commitment, and talent. Virginia loved her Friday morning art class and still does to this day.

I once asked her how she felt about Artworks Studio. She told me it was a great learning and life experience for her. Her art skills developed to such a high level in large part due to her involvement in Artworks Studio. Teaching has always been one of the best ways of learning.

She told me, "The friends I make along the way are incredible and bring great comfort and joy. I rarely feel like I'm going to work; more like I am going to play."

I asked her, "When are you going to retire?"

She answered, "Never!"

Virginia's Legacy

Art instruction helps children with the development of a number of skills including hand/eye coordination, visual perception, high self-esteem, art appreciation, and creativity. Virginia encouraged the development of those skills in thousands of students through her 35 plus years of instruction. If that were all she provided, her legacy would be secure. But there was so much more. She provided love, humor, and a safe and healthy environment where they could share their stories on and off the canvas.

Virginia has sold paintings throughout the country and here in Santa Clarita. She's held many exhibits and donated several of her paintings to charity. I am very, very proud of her.

CHAPTER TEN

THE BARCODE YEARS

Council Chambers

After ten more speakers, most of whom I did not know, I continued to be impressed by the level of competition for the appointment. I'm sure each one felt they could serve on the council and probably do a good job. The decision to be made by the council that night was not going to be easy. I wondered what motivated so many people to apply for the position.

Service is a strong motivator. I suspect most candidates wanted to serve the community. Power is another motivator. Some candidates, sadly, sought what they perceived was the power of the office of councilmember. Others looked at income. It was a paying position, very modest at less than $25,000 per year, but for some it was enough.

Did they know that council decisions required a majority vote of the council? One person could not solve the transportation, homeless, and veterans' problems in our city. Each required consensus. If I had one serious criticism of the candidate presentations, it would be the failure of many to address the consensus issue and the importance of having the ability to build consensus.

Another issue was having the ability to understand and work within a budget of about $200,000,000. Because Santa Clarita is a very big city, it requires large sums of money for everything that it does. How the council allocated that money was critical to the direction of the city. Councilmembers did not manage home budgets or small business budgets. They managed millions of dollars for one of the largest cities in the country.

Still another issue seemingly ignored was education and the schools. City government does not control the schools. School districts control the schools. Councilmembers can advocate for school issues, but they have no direct control of the schools. Some candidates didn't understand that and spoke as if education was their platform.

One candidate admitted he did not know what the job of a councilmember entailed but said he would perform it to the best of his abilities. He was humorous in his presentation and the audience laughter provided a welcome relief from the pressure of the night. And with that, I went back to drifting and I thought about barcodes.

Computer Identics

In the mid '80s, I left the fast and furious world of Data General and made a huge career change. I went from a Fortune 500 company in an industry I knew well, to a small $8,000,000 barcode company, Computer Identics, in an industry I knew nothing about.

Computer Identics was run by some of the brightest barcode gurus in the industry. They taught me the industry from the ground up. It took a while and lots of frustrating hard work, but before long I became knowledgeable enough to lead their sales force. I traveled the country making barcode presentations and, with a great support team, helped to grow the company over four years from

$8,000,000 to almost $30,000,000 in sales as the company's Director of Sales and Marketing.

Our team included a regional manager, Joe Frustaci, who had little management experience but could sell like no one I knew. Joe Frustaci, a New Jersey Italian-American with Sicilian ancestry, was able to take his sales skills, use them to manage other people, and make his region number one in the country. His team landed huge multi-million dollar accounts including UPS and FedEx. In large part, Joe and his team led the way to our growth in sales and the success of my time at Computer Identics. Thank you Joe!

In the Midwest, I had a different kind of regional manager. Where Joe Frustaci was a people person extraordinaire, my Midwest manager was a computer geek. He was good at pitching our products, but not a good closer. That's where I came in.

This is a story of one of the fastest turnarounds in my sales career. It was also one of the most amazing. In less than 24 hours we went from losing a million dollar deal to winning it.

We had a million dollar deal go south on us in Green Bay, Wisconsin. I was in San Francisco when I spoke with our president by phone. He told me we lost the deal. The presentation they were given by our techie didn't go well and the company in Green Bay called to tell him they were going to sign with our competitor the next day. The deal was dead. I was shocked. Our company could run circles over the competition and should have won that deal easily. Something was wrong and I was going to fix it. I immediately went into action.

I called the president of the company in Green Bay and asked him to allow me to make another presentation in the morning. I told him that our company could solve his problems better, faster and more economically than our competitor. He told me it was too late. He was signing with the competitor in the morning. I told him our team had worked many months to put together our proposal and we deserved at least one last hearing, even if only for an hour. He reluctantly agreed to give us an hour. He scheduled us at 9:00 a.m. He said we had exactly one hour. The competitor would be there at 10:00 a.m. and he was going to sign with them. Even though it looked bleak, we had a chance.

I was in San Francisco; my techie team was in Boston and the company in question was in Green Bay. It was 2:00 p.m. my time and 5:00 p.m. Boston time. I called my techies, got them to agree to put a revised presentation together and meet me in Detroit in the morning for the short flight to Green Bay.

I took a redeye from San Francisco and arrived in Detroit just after dawn. I found a hotel at the airport. I went in, went up to the third floor rooms and walked up to where a maid was cleaning a room. I told her I'd give her $10 if I could take a shower in the room she was cleaning. She reluctantly agreed. I showered and dressed in my best business suit and tie. When I met up with the other three men they were amazed that I looked like I just got out of a shower. I told them I did and we all laughed.

The four of us took a commuter plane to Green Bay. We rented a car and went over our presentation as we drove to the company. At exactly 9:00 a.m. everyone was in place. The president walked in; he was alone. Normally executives bring a team of advisers with them to presentations. He didn't. That was a bad sign.

He reminded us that we only had an hour and that we should be very brief and concise. Our presentation began. I reminded the president of all the reasons why his company needed a state of the art barcoding system in order to compete in his industry. I asked him to tell me what parts of our proposal he had doubts about and why he felt the competitor could do better.

The president spoke for about 30 minutes and told us of his reservations. When he was done I told him we could address every reservation positively if we had more time. I told him I brought my best technical people with me and they were prepared to meet with his best technical people, right then and there, to prove our ability to give his company the system they wanted.

I must have been convincing because at 10:00 a.m. the president's administrator entered the conference room and said the competitor had arrived. The president told her to ask them to come back at lunchtime. Then he told her to send in his technical advisers. About a half dozen of them came in and all of sudden we had a "techie fest."

At lunchtime the administrator came in again with the same message. He told her to ask them to come back at 2:00 p.m. and to order some sandwiches for us. We were on a roll. The techies on both sides were in their glory. They filled a white board with so much info and so many diagrams that they ran out of space. After hours of techie-to-techie conversation, everyone stopped, smiled, and told us they were very happy. The president smiled too.

At 2:00 p.m., he and I shook hands on a million dollar deal. As my team and I walked out of the building we saw the competitor team sitting annoyed in the lobby. We smiled at them. They frowned at us. We got into our rental car. On the drive back to the airport we passed Lambeau Field. We stopped, got out of the car and celebrated our victory by jumping up and down and howling at the stadium. Curly Lambeau and Vince Lombardi would have been proud.

ScanMex

In my last year at Computer Identics we planned to expand internationally. Europe was the favored region. I favored Mexico. Europe was more advanced in barcode technology and competition was stiff. Plus, the cost of entry into that arena was very high compared to Mexico. I presented my case with an in depth business plan for taking our company into Mexico. Others presented the plan for Europe. They won out. Computer Identics was not going to enter the barcode industry in Mexico. But I was.

I showed Virginia my business plan. She was tepid at first because she wasn't sure about me going to Mexico and leaving her and teenage Eva for weeks at a time. But as I described the plan to her, she could feel my passion for it. She had been with me for 20 years and she knew me. If I felt I had a winner, my passion for the project would consume me. She asked a lot of questions and only when she felt satisfied with the answers did she agree to go along with the plan. Best of all, she became passionate about the project and went to work helping me.

I found two prospective partners in the industry who could help me get started. Things sounded good initially, but during the six months of preparation and research that followed, it became evident the partnership was not going to work. I was on my own. Except for Virginia. She helped name the company, designed its logo and business cards, and prepared me mentally the travails of starting a new business. When the time came, we were excited and scared. As I left for my first business trip to Mexico City, Virginia told me to be careful and to call her before making any significant decisions.

I hugged her, kissed her, and said, "Don't worry. What could go wrong?"

Of all the adventures I've had in my life, that one had to be the craziest. First, a little background. I'm a "Nuyorican." That's a Puerto Rican from New York City. Our Spanish is not quite pure. We usually don't roll our R's as much and often don't pronounce the last letters of a word. We also have our own unique idioms that may mean nothing to other Spanish speakers. All of that is important to know and understand before starting a business in Mexico. I must have forgotten that part. I just assumed a Latino was a Latino anywhere I went.

When I got to Mexico City it hit me that I didn't know a soul there. I had the company name, ScanMex, and nothing else except the cockiness to expect to be treated like a business executive, even though I didn't have a business yet. I stayed in a hotel in the Zona Rosa, a nice touristy place. In the morning I went to the dining room for breakfast. When the waiter asked for my order, I told him I wanted a tortilla. He asked what I wanted with my tortilla and I told him I wasn't very hungry and that just a tortilla would do. He looked at me a little strange and asked if I wanted flour or corn.

"I don't want flour or corn," I replied. "Just a tortilla."

Scratching his head, he asked if I wanted something to drink. "Jugo de china," I said.

He'd had enough. "Excuse me, sir. I get that you're not hungry. You ordered a tortilla and now you don't want a tortilla. I can get you the juice you want but it may take a while if I have to go to China to get it." Funny guy.

To a Puerto Rican, a tortilla is an omelet. I thought I was ordering an omelet and he thought I was ordering a slice of bread, right? I wanted an orange juice. In Puerto Rico, an orange juice is called jugo de china, juice from China. Don't ask me why. That's just what it's called.

So, right away, I knew this wasn't going to be easy. I finished breakfast and headed back to my room to make my first phone calls. It was game time. I brushed my teeth and turned the television on for background noise. Whoa, Baywatch was on. No self-respecting American man is going to pass on watching Baywatch, so I watched it.

When it ended I thumbed through the yellow pages and made a list of companies to call. By then it was noon and I was hungry. I discovered that lunch in Mexico tends to run from 1:00 – 3:00 p.m. So I sat in the lobby waiting for the restaurant to open, reading the newspaper and acting like I was doing something constructive.

Lunch in Mexico is an event. The waiter comes slowly and the food comes even slower. But everything is wonderful and the scenery's wonderful and life is good. And now it's

3:00 p.m. and all I've done is eat breakfast, lunch and watch Baywatch. I was not off to a good start.

As a side note: for those of you who dream of starting a business, just know that you've got to have high energy, a lot of accomplishments and the ability to get things done. Please note that does not include watching Baywatch. I was stalling badly. It was obvious I had lost my confidence. Making cold calls to Mexican businesses was going to be extremely difficult for me. I wasn't sure I belonged anymore. I was questioning whether I'd made a mistake thinking I could come to Mexico to start a business.

And then I thought about Virginia. She helped me so much with my plan. She was as excited about our venture as I was and she was counting on me to succeed. She didn't expect me to return two days later with my tail between my legs. So I sucked it up and determined to succeed.

I started with the easiest call I could make. It was to the American Embassy. They directed me to the American Chamber of Commerce right near my hotel. I went there and met with a representative who was very cordial and informative. She told me I arrived just at the right time.

Mexico had just started a barcode association for the purpose of studying how to introduce barcodes into their industries. A barcode trade show was starting in two days, but the absolute deadline to register was 7:00 p.m. that afternoon in Polanco on the other side of Mexico City. It was already 5:00 p.m.. She was sure I couldn't make it in time. "The traffic is too heavy during rush hour. You might want to reconsider," she said apologetically. "I'll make it," I insisted. "Just tell me where I have to go."

She gave me the information and called ahead to let them know to expect me. I thanked her, rushed out of her office, found the Metro and took it to the address she gave me. I got there a little after 6:00 p.m.. I introduced myself to the head of the barcode association who asked how I had gotten there so fast. I told her I took the Metro. She said, "You took the Metro? You should never have done that!" I asked her why not and she said, "Look at you. You're an American in a business suit. You're a prime target for robbers and kidnappers."

Two things hit me between the eyes. The first was her identifying me as an American so easily. There I was trying to blend in with the Mexicans and instead I stood out like a sore thumb. Ugh! The other was her use of the words robbers and kidnappers. What? Gulp.

She told me Mexico needed people who could help them learn how barcodes could benefit their country. She was thrilled someone with my barcode knowledge had arrived. She said my timing was perfect. The association was holding a convention for industries to share the little barcode knowledge that they had. She said if I could attend I would be surrounded by many business professionals who wanted to learn more. I was more than happy to oblige.

At the convention, I found myself surrounded by many business leaders wanting to know what the latest barcode applications were and how to implement them. I answered many questions and I asked a lot too. It was a good exchange of knowledge. As I expected, they were a few years behind the U.S. in barcoding. I walked around the convention asking people what they thought was needed to successfully bring barcode systems to Mexico. I got some great ideas from them.

A gray haired man with rimless glasses and a broad smile was exhibiting very basic bar code systems. As I walked past, he beckoned me to visit his display. He told me he was a professor at the Universidad La Salle, A.C. His name was Pepe Cajigas. I took Professor Cajigas for a cup of coffee and told him about wanting to start ScanMex. He could tell I was serious and decided to help by giving me some much needed advice. The first thing he suggested was that I hire a Mexican computer engineer. He also advised that I needed a Mexican citizen to create a Mexican corporation and I needed a computer engineer to implement my barcode systems. He had access to many former student engineers and all were Mexican citizens. He offered to help me recruit one. I liked Pepe. I was very comfortable around him. He was upbeat, cheerful, and at the same time very knowledgeable. He became my trusted adviser.

Later that evening we had tequila together and shared war stories of our computer experiences. We laughed and drank and drank and laughed. After a while his wife, and then a few of his students, joined us. It was a full-blown fiesta.

A couple of weeks later, he hooked me up with Alejandro Molina, who turned out to be the perfect person for ScanMex. Alejandro was one of Pepe's ex-students. He was in his early 30s and had started his own systems company. He was only just learning about barcode systems. We had a breakfast interview and I hired him on the spot. He was brilliant, personable, and could sell.

The two of us then built the company from that start. Here's how we did it.

First we got an office. We searched all over for a good bargain price at a decent location. We found one in the Colonia del Valle district in an office building along a main thoroughfare close to the Metro. It was 300-square-feet with a tiny reception area, an even smaller tech area, and a microscopic manager's office. We had one phone and it was in the reception area. To answer the phone, we needed a receptionist. Alejandro took care of that. He knew a talented lady who worked for next to nothing. We hired her. She handled the one or two calls a day that dribbled in, while Alejandro and I were out making as many sales calls as we could muster. One was to Correos de Mexico, the post office system of Mexico. They agreed to let us put 1,000 scanners into their mail system if we would give them away free.

"Just think," I was told. "People all over Mexico will see your scanners. We are offering you free advertising."

We respectfully declined.

Another sales call was to a large department store. They, too, wanted free scanners. Again, we declined. But then we finally got lucky.

I was at the airport killing time waiting for a flight home at a duty free store when I noticed that none of the items on their shelves were barcoded. I asked the manager if they used barcode systems and he said no. I took his name and gave it to Alejandro for a potential sales follow-up. He followed through and it only took a couple of weeks to get our very first sale. It was large enough to pay our rent for a few months, but not our receptionist. We were still in the red. But not for long.

I made a sales call to a large delivery services company called Estafeta. They were considered the FedEx of Mexico. They told me they had a huge problem. Customers complained their packages were not delivered on time, if at all. They told me they knew that UPS in the U.S. had a good system of tracking packages and they were looking for something similar. I told them I was involved in the UPS project and knew it well. I suggested they could have a better system than UPS's because we had newer technology now. It took a few months of demonstrating our technology to them, but in the end they loved it.

It took another few weeks of negotiating price, before we reached a dead end. Neither of us would budge. At our final meeting, Estafeta's CEO told me to sharpen my pencil. I told him that I'd sharpened it as much as I could and reminded him that I wasn't in the business of losing money on my sales. He reminded me that I could lose the sale. I finished my part of the conversation by telling him that he was losing customers every day and because of that he could end up losing his job. And with that, ScanMex had its first million-dollar customer.

We rented a bigger office and hired some technical people and a full-time administrator. We got a real phone system and saved the first one to someday go into the

ScanMex museum. We had a real company. It was exhilarating. I couldn't wait to get home to share the news with Virginia. When I did she felt happy and sad at the same time. We had a successful new business, but my travels would keep us apart much more than we expected.

I commuted to Mexico from Santa Clarita for almost five years. During that time, Alejandro and I built ScanMex into the number one barcode systems company in Mexico. We got so big we bought our own building to house our crew and equipment. But I was becoming tired of all the travel and gave less and less to ScanMex. Eventually the day came when I'd had enough and I sold my shares in the company to Alejandro. He got a great deal, and finally, I could stay at home with my family. It was a win-win.

CHAPTER ELEVEN

BMC, STROKE & RECOVERY

My Turn

The Mayor was down to the final few speakers. My turn was coming up very soon. I no longer had the luxury to drift away. I had to be in the moment. Focus. Deliver.

A few minutes later it was my turn. The Mayor announced the final speaker. "Batting cleanup, Mr. Miranda. Bill Miranda." I could almost hear my wife, mother, father, and brother saying in unison, "You got this Willie."

I made my way to the podium and began to speak. I spoke passionately about Santa Clarita and how amazing it is. I told them that I moved here 34 years before with my wife and two youngest daughters, and that I'd been a Fortune 500 business executive, an entrepreneur, and a community leader over the course of my time here. I spoke about my non-profit experiences helping small business owners, veterans, seniors and the homeless. I told them I wanted to keep Santa Clarita an amazing place well into the future. I mentioned how my business background would make it possible for me to help attract new businesses to Santa Clarita. I told them that I'm a veteran and understand many of their needs and am compassionate to them.

Finally, I mentioned that I wanted to roll up my sleeves to help those less fortunate. I wanted to help them in any way I could. I ended by telling the council, "You have a tough decision to make tonight. I wish you well. Thank you." With that, the presentations were done, and the council went into a short recess. I was relieved. My presentation was done. I felt I had delivered it as best as I could. I was satisfied. Now it was up to the council. The recess gave me more time to reflect on my career.

Bill Miranda Consulting

After I sold ScanMex I became a business consultant. I consulted for large companies all over the world. I had three clients in Switzerland, two in Germany and one each in England, France, Holland and Belgium. In Asia, I had clients in Taiwan and China. Most of those clients came to me via my barcode connections but they did not necessarily want barcode consulting. Some wanted to tap into my broad experience in international business.

It was incredible. I traveled all over the world. I took Virginia with me on my first Asian trip. My clients treated her like a queen. Everywhere we went, Tokyo, Hong Kong, Shenzhen and Shanghai, I spent the day with clients while she and her driver escorts went sightseeing and shopping. In the evenings, my clients always arranged a fancy dinner that included Virginia.

I thought about the time in Taiwan, in the capital city of Taipei, when Virginia was too tired to join us for dinner. A day of heavy sightseeing and shopping will do that to you. We were in a wonderful hotel suite and she just wanted to take a long bath while I had dinner with my clients. I kissed her goodbye and reminded her that there was a phone by the tub if Her Highness should need anything.

I met my clients in the dining suite and immediately apologized for my wife not being there. I said that Mrs. Miranda was very tired from a long day. The eight other men in the room each smiled and nodded that they understood. We chatted and drank for half an hour before we sat down for dinner. Nobody spoke. No server entered the room. Everyone stared at their plates, except me. Five minutes, then ten minutes went by. Realizing something was wrong; I asked what the problem was. "We are waiting for Mrs. Miranda," was the reply. I mentioned Mrs. Miranda was probably sleeping by now. They answered that they would wait and went back to staring at their plates. I excused myself and made my way to the phone.

"Hello, Darling," Virginia answered. "I hope all is going well downstairs because this tub is absolutely divine."

"Uh, we have a problem," I answered. I told her there were eight men staring at their plates who refused to eat until she joined us. Thirty minutes later, as beautiful as ever, Virginia walked into the dining room. The men were very happy to see her. They stood, bowed very politely and waited until she sat down before they took their seats. Immediately, the servers arrived with the food. Each man took turns speaking with Virginia while the others listened closely. I was invisible to them. Virginia had that effect on people.

Virginia and Bill in Heidelberg Germany

The Stroke

All the traveling finally took its toll on me. One month I was in Europe and the next in Asia. I had set up an office in South Torrance because that was where my biggest client was headquartered. In between international trips, I commuted to Torrance on I-405, one of the busiest roads to travel in Los Angeles. On Friday, February 7, 2003, I called Virginia from my Torrance office at 2:00 p.m..

"Sweetheart, great news. I'm a little tired. I'm coming home early today. I'm not going to wait for rush hour," I told her.

She was very happy to hear that. Virginia said, "Your dad is at the mall shopping. He is also going to be happy to see you early." My father was visiting from New York.

I told my administrator she could go home early too and asked her how I could help her get ready to go. She said she would shut down her computer and would be ready to go, but if I wanted to help I could run downstairs to grab the mail. No problem. I ran downstairs and felt good enough to jog back up. When I got to the top step I felt a very sharp pain in the back of my neck and fell forward onto the landing. I remember falling forward. I don't remember crawling, but I'm told that I crawled to the door and banged on it. My administrator saw me lying on the floor. She immediately called 911. The paramedics arrived within eight minutes and I was in intensive care at Little Company of Mary Hospital shortly thereafter. I was in a coma. I'd had a stroke.

It was Sunday evening when I came out of it. I opened my eyes, looked around and saw a tearful Virginia staring at me. Behind her were my three daughters and my father. I was attached to wires and tubes. I couldn't remember how I got there.

Two weeks later, after good medical care and lots of love from the family, I left the hospital and went home. My body was relatively undamaged, but my brain was not. My speech was extremely slow as was almost every movement I made. Everybody was worried, including me.

The Recovery

The first year of my recovery was spent on the couch in the family room staring at the TV. I'm not sure that I ever really watched it. I just stared at it and Virginia fed me my meals. Ever so slowly, I was able to speak a little more coherently. Then I regained the use of my arms and fingers. Eventually, I could walk and get myself up and down. One day, I guess I was feeling extra good, I ventured out for a walk on my own. For the next 250 days, come rain or shine, I walked.

Virginia ran the household, the art studio and took care of me. She did her best to take care of our finances. Even with medical insurance, a two-week hospital stay can be economically crushing. Added to that, I no longer had an income. I'm still not sure how we survived my two years of recovery but I credit most of it to Virginia.

Two years into recovery I appeared to be 100 percent but I wasn't. There was that pesky 5 percent that was invisible to most people. It was in my dexterity and balance. Once in a while I had some dizziness but overall I was good. As a spiritual person, I really believe in the power of prayer. I prayed to the Lord every day, "Lord, I know it's your will that matters and not mine, but if you want my input, I think I'm worth saving a little longer."

After two years of no income, I needed to find work. Not the work I was accustomed to, but less stressful work that I could do without traveling or commuting. I went to a Farmers Insurance seminar and ended up starting my own Farmers Insurance agency. Farmers trained me well and my agency got off to a decent start. It was hard work. It was more work than I was really willing to put into it. As much as I wanted to succeed at the agency, I could tell well into the second year that it just wasn't going to be something that I wanted to continue doing. I wasn't even sure I had the ability to continue. So, I gave up my Farmer's agency and went back to consulting.

The best thing that came from my two years at Farmers was a dear and lasting friendship with Marlon Roa. That friendship made my time at Farmers well worth it. Marlon is a Latino who champions Latino causes. Just being around him reminded me that I could do so much more to help our Latino community.

I joined the Small Business Development Center. I worked with a lot of small businesses throughout my two years there. I was the only Spanish-speaking counselor in our center so I worked with many Latino small businesses. They needed help; more help than the center could give them. That's when I decided to form the SCV Latino Chamber of Commerce. Marlon Roa was by my side and together we were going to make a difference.

The Daughters Support Team

CHAPTER TWELVE

SCV LATINO CHAMBER OF COMMERCE

Council Chambers

The council was still at recess. Candidates and their supporters were up and about socializing while we waited for the council to return. The meeting was down to the short strokes. They had narrowed it down to a handful of candidates, then the council would ask them an unknown number of questions. That was to be followed by councilmember deliberation and hopefully a decision on whom to appoint.

I didn't mix and mingle. I sat in my chair staring at the empty chair on the dais wondering if I would be the one to fill it. If appointed, that would be a new experience for me. It would be a new adventure. The appointment was to complete Dante Acosta's term, which meant it was for a little less than two years. If I were appointed and wanted to run for a full term, I would only have a year to learn the ropes of the job before having to run for reelection. Lots to learn in a short period of time in order to achieve the success intended. It reminded me of when I started the SCV Latino Chamber of Commerce.

SCV Latino Chamber

My experience with the Small Business Development Center taught me that there were many Latino small business owners in our city. Some of them needed more help than the SBDC offered. Many Latino owners spoke English, but they felt more comfortable speaking Spanish, especially when discussing their businesses. For whatever reason, the SCV Chamber of Commerce wasn't considered Latino-friendly at the time. It only made sense then, to start a Latino Chamber of Commerce. With the strong support of Marlon Roa and others who championed Latino causes, we started the Latino Chamber of Commerce. Our goal was to engage Latino business owners and their families, and to help promote their businesses.

We didn't have much money, so we had to learn quickly. We knew that Latinos tended to do business differently. Normally we didn't dive in with elevator speeches or business card exchanges. Instead we give an abrazo (hug) and asked about each other's family. It was just our greeting. At events we expected and enjoyed food, music, and given the right environment, dancing. We considered everyone a friend. Everyone was welcomed into our homes.

There was a protocol that we followed. It was an informal protocol but a protocol, nonetheless. First we greeted each other properly, and then we talked about our families. Then we would move on to the weather and our homes. It was not until all the small talk occurred that we began talking business. It may have taken a little longer, but our loyalty lasted for years and helped us overcome many challenges.

We wanted to make a big splash in the community. We wanted to hold big events to introduce all the members of our community to Latino businesses. The first event we participated in was the Latino Business Expo. It was the idea of our good friends, Lee Cadena and Judith Cassis. It was held at the community's best venue, the Hyatt Regency Valencia grand ballroom. The event was fantastic. Dozens of

Latino businesses got a chance to show their products and services to hundreds of attendees. We followed that up with a huge Cinco de Mayo event on Main Street in Old Town Newhall. That had never been done before. We worked with the city staff and our members to make it happen. Some members weren't sure it was a good idea but the event was a huge success and they were very happy. Because of its success, we held the celebration on Main Street for the following five years.

We organized another summer event at William S. Hart Park called, Viva La Salsa! There were orchestras, professional salsa dancers, an area for public dancing, and lots of food. Hundreds attended. Virginia, who is a crazy good dancer, danced with me until late into the night. People are amazed at how much energy we have. I think it's because we're in love and that energizes us. The event was another huge success and it ran for three years.

Our feature event, held annually for eight years at the Hyatt Regency Valencia, was the Latino Chamber Gala. Latino business owners and their families decked out in tuxedos, fancy gowns and jewelry. We celebrated ourselves, gave out awards and always had a keynote speaker. Of course great food, music, and dancing was central. It became one of Santa Clarita's can't miss events. We packed the grand ballroom every year. Attendees always included local celebrities and elected officials, as well as heads of our largest organizations, businesses, government, and non-profits.

After eight very successful years, and a very positive management change at the SCV Chamber of Commerce, we decided to merge back in with them. It wasn't an easy decision. Some board members fought the merger, but in the end it was the right thing to do.

As part of the merger agreement, Latinos gained three seats on the SCV Chamber's board of directors. We had a seat at the table. Thanks to the chamber's new management team, we also had a say at the table. The chamber, with our advocacy, formed the Latino Business Alliance and made it an advocacy group for the Latino business community. Latinos became an integral part of the chamber.

Our Valley Magazine

During the Latino chamber years I began working as an adviser to a small group of creative people who started a bi-lingual magazine called, Our Valleys/Nuestros Valles. It was the brainchild of Francisco Del Rio, his son Julio, and Julio's wife, Patsy Ayala. There were other partners who were instrumental in starting the magazine, but the Del Rio family eventually became the sole owners. I bought into the company and became the fourth owner.

The magazine was a labor of love. Although we barely broke even financially, we delivered the magazine to thousands of homes in Santa Clarita every month for eight years. Our content included articles that featured multiculturalism, diversity, and inclusion. We stressed those things in every issue. The chamber members loved us, especially since we helped promote their businesses and our culture. Naturally, Virginia designed most of our covers, many of which featured her paintings

Radio Shows

While working with the magazine, Patsy Ayala and I created a weekly talk show we called, Querer es Poder, translated it meant, "where there's a will there's a way." Our guests included many Latino leaders in our community as well as most public officials, business executives, and non-profit leaders. Carl and Jeri Seratti-Goldman, the owners of our local Hometown Station, KHTS 1220, AM & FM, were very helpful in putting our show together. They taught us everything we know about broadcasting and the use of media. We broadcasted the program every week for two years.

Profiles in Latino Courage

I really loved hearing the stories of my Latino friends and how they overcame great obstacles to achieve success. I decided to write a book highlighting seven of those stories. Writing a book was a lot more difficult than I thought it would be. First, I had to decide what stories to write. Then I had to gather information from each person. Next, I had to write the stories in an interesting narrative and, finally, I had to get the book edited, formatted, and published. With lots of help, I was able to do it all in nine months. The book, *Profiles in Latino Courage*, was published in 2013. It wasn't a best seller, but it sold well enough for me. I enjoyed the many book signings we held. They afforded me the opportunity to meet some interesting people who were gracious enough to share their personal stories with me.

Feeling Our Roots

Cinco de Mayo Celebration

Questions and Deliberation

When the council returned from its recess, they called on about a dozen candidates to answer some questions. I was the last one of those called. I went to the podium and Mayor Pro Tem Weste asked me if I had voted in recent elections. I said I had voted in every election since I was 21-years-old. She then asked how I was able to merge the Santa Clarita Valley Latino Chamber of Commerce and the Santa Clarita Valley Chamber of Commerce. I answered that it wasn't easy. There were people on both sides that basically wouldn't budge in the discussion to merge or not merge. I told the council that I was able to work with both chambers to convince each of them of the benefits to be derived from combining their efforts. Not everyone involved was happy, but in the end, we built a consensus.

The Mayor Pro Tem continued, "Tell me a little bit about bringing jobs to Santa Clarita."

I told her that the city needed to work with the Santa Clarita Valley Economic Development Corporation to put the word out that Santa Clarita is a business friendly community, and that there were many skilled workers here who enjoy living in a family oriented environment. With all my high-level business experience, I said I could be very helpful in those efforts.

The Mayor Pro Tem then mentioned that I was a veteran and worked with seniors. She wanted to know how I handled working with so many non-profits. I told her I was honored to serve those people in need. I also told her that my 95-year-old mother-in-law wanted me to mention that she attended the senior center three times a week. In fact, when she was in her early eighties, she met her boyfriend there. That got a huge laugh from everyone.

Next Councilmember Marsha McLean asked me about my ideas to get more civic engagement in our community. She mentioned that most people say they just don't have enough time to be involved. I told her I felt not having enough time is often just an excuse. When something is important enough, we find the time to do it. To engage others in civic duties, we have to make it important enough for them. I added that it took a lot of people, engaged civically, to build our Newhall Community Center and our Old Town Newhall Library. Both have made a tremendous difference in our under-served communities and are major centers for education and recreation in Old Town Newhall.

Mayor Smyth mentioned that I'd just made the deadline with only two hours to spare.

"Was that an indication of hesitancy on your part?" He asked.

I answered, "Absolutely not."

"Do you have enough time to serve on the council since you are involved with so many non-profit boards?" asked the Mayor.

"The city council is the biggest board of all. I will give up the other board positions for a council seat, as that will allow me the opportunity to help the most people," I replied.

With that the questioning was complete. All that was needed now was a council discussion, a nomination, a second, and a vote. And there can only be one.

CHAPTER THIRTEEN

COUNCIL YEARS 1 & 2

The Nomination and Appointment

It was time for the council to get to the heart of the matter and make the appointment. One could hear a pin drop in the room as all awaited the council's decision. Councilmember Bob Kellar spoke first and gave a glowing endorsement of candidate Brent Braun. I knew Brent would be competing with me at the very end. It was obvious he was going to get Councilmember Kellar's vote. Marsha McLean went next and mentioned a few people kindly, but said she was homed in on Bill Miranda. She felt I was good at helping bring the community together. Mayor Pro Tem Laurene Weste mentioned a few people kindly, but said she was very impressed with the work I had done with non-profits. She said I was very gentle with people and that is a good quality to have.

At that point I felt like I had two yes votes (McLean and Weste) and one no vote (Kellar). The whole ball of wax depended on Mayor Cameron Smyth. The tension in the room got stronger. It took three votes to win the seat. If I got only two votes I would lose. Cameron was the decider.

He spoke, "Both Brent Braun and Bill Miranda are outstanding candidates. I could support either one. If you wanted to go in a different direction, I could go with Dr. Dwork. She's an outstanding candidate too."

My heart sank. Cameron had just introduced what I considered to be the third option. I was hoping that only Brent Braun and I would be the finalists. Cameron could have chosen one of us but introducing Dr. Dwork at the very last moment was not what I had hoped. She was a formidable competitor in my eyes.

Mayor Pro Tem Weste volunteered that she was still most impressed by me and that she was nominating me to be the appointee. Councilmember Marsha McLean quickly seconded the motion. Mayor Smyth called on the city clerk to take the vote. The tension in the room could not have been thicker.

At that moment I almost wanted to be somewhere else, anywhere else. There was no time for reminiscing. There was no time for contemplation. The time was now and there could only be one.

Mary Cusick, the City Clerk, called the roll. "Councilmember Kellar?"

"No. I like Bill Miranda. He is a friend and a good man, but I have to go with someone else."

"Councilmember McLean?" "Yes."

"Mayor Pro Tem Weste?" "Aye."

"Mayor Smyth?"

The Mayor paused for what felt like a lifetime. I could almost feel Virginia holding her breath, my mother praying, my father encouraging and my brother's arm around me. And then the Mayor voted. "Aye."

Everyone applauded as the Mayor said, "Congratulations, Mr. Miranda."

After accepting congratulations from everyone there, I rushed home to tell Virginia the good news. I pulled in the garage and took a moment alone in my car to pray. "Dear Lord, thank you for giving me this opportunity to serve my city and my community. I pledge to do the very best I possibly can to be worthy. I cannot do this without You. Please guide me. Amen."

I bolted out of the car and rushed into the house. Virginia came running toward me with a big hug. I asked her how she knew and she said she'd already received many phone calls of congrats. We celebrated with a glass of wine, tequila, or maybe both. We were very excited, and I don't know that either one of us slept well that night. It was time for the real adventure to begin.

Year One: Learning the Ropes

I received the appointment on the 17th of January and I was sworn in on the 24th. Virginia was by my side. The City of Santa Clarita is among the top 100 or so cities in population in the U.S. It's the eighteenth largest city in California. With 235,000 residents, it's the third largest city in L.A. County behind Los Angeles and Long Beach. Joining its council was a big deal.

One of the first issues I addressed on the council was multiculturalism. The other members were very supportive. Immediately after taking the seat, I called for a proclamation by honoring and celebrating Black History Month. We also adopted a resolution reaffirming Santa Clarita's commitment to a diverse, supportive, and inclusive community. Later, we proclaimed Hispanic Heritage Month and Filipino Heritage Month, as well as Senior Center Month and Homeless Awareness Month. My goal was not just to make proclamations, but also to bring awareness to the diverse needs of our community.

Arts and Entertainment are important to me as well. One can judge a society by the level of importance it gives to the arts. Santa Clarita has always done well with the arts, but when I joined the council there were some important needs. We addressed those needs immediately. I pushed for and raised support to keep Old Town Newhall as a designated arts and entertainment district only, as opposed to allowing new businesses not associated with arts and entertainment. I voted to take over The Main Theater and keep it safe for the arts when it was about to go under. I voted additional funding to complete the Newhall Family Theater for the Performing Arts. It helped to complete the restoration of a special historic theater in Old Town Newhall. I have to give a special shout out here to Councilmember Laurene Weste. She literally took me by the hand and walked me through the theater explaining the details of its historic significance.

I didn't just talk the talk. I walked the walk. I was one of the lead characters in the Canyon Theatre Guild performances of Willy Wonka. I was Mr. Salt thanks to Laurie

Morgan, the show's director. The show ran for a month and opened shortly after I became a councilmember. Instead of my first public appearance being a groundbreaking or other celebration, it was on stage as the arrogant father, Mr. Salt, of a spoiled child, Veruca. It was so much fun.

Veterans' issues have always been very near and dear to me. As an Air Force veteran, I want to do all I can to support our veterans. The late Bill Reynolds, the head of the Fallen Veterans Monument committee, approached me on the issue of completing the project. It had been stalled for reasons I didn't understand. I supported completing it, and with the unanimous vote of the council, we got it done. I also voted to give $350,000 to Habitat for Humanity, an organization that builds housing for veterans and their families.

Our job on the council is to help our citizens avoid homelessness and to address the issues people face who find themselves in that vulnerable position. We supported the organizations that were working with the homeless. The primary shelter was Bridge to Home. The city has given considerable funds to Bridge to Home for land, temporary shelter, etc. With some extra funding from the County of Los Angeles, Bridge to Home was able to offer homeless shelter year round, instead of for just a few months of the year.

Seniors are near and dear to me. I made sure I visited the senior center on a regular basis to support them in any way I could. I contributed to the building of the new senior center both with my vote on the council and with my own personal funds, which I donated in the name of my mother-in-law.

The most emotional moment I experienced on the council was when we resolved the issue over manufactured home rental procedures. Some of the owners of manufactured home parks wanted to change the way they did business. They wanted to decrease the number of 55 and over homes and increase the number of general public homes that came with no rent controls, so they could charge a lot more. In addition, the owners wanted to raise the rents of the seniors beyond what had previously been agreed. I'm generalizing a bit here in order to make the issue easily understandable, but I'm sure you get the gist.

Seniors living in the parks flocked to our council meetings pleading with us to save them from being forced out of their homes. They claimed that even a modest rent increase for those on fixed incomes was akin to an eviction notice. After months of fact gathering and hearing from both sides of the issue, the council voted in favor of the seniors. When the council meeting adjourned, seniors came up to the council and thanked us. They were so grateful. It took everything I had to keep myself from crying as they expressed their appreciation through teary eyes.

Midway through the year I came up with the idea of doing a television show, "SCV 101," on public television (SCVTV). Thanks to station CEO, Leon Worden, I was able to pull it together. The show highlighted the goings on in our community. My first guest was City Manager Ken Striplin, and over time I interviewed most of the city's key officials on the show, as well as many of the local movers and shakers. The show continues and is starting its fifth year.

My first year on the council was a great learning experience. The majority of people were supportive of my work. A few were highly critical. Some were very insulting.

That comes with the job. Don't do it if you don't have thick skin.

Year Two: Year of Decisions

There were three events that rocked my world in year two: the "sanctuary city" debate, the 2020 election campaign, and my daughter Eva's cancer diagnosis.

Sanctuary City Debate

Senate Bill 54 (SB54), the sanctuary state bill, passed in Sacramento in 2017. The bill was designed to prevent local law enforcement agencies from detaining undocumented immigrants who are eligible for deportation by ICE for violating immigration laws. The only exceptions were those who had been convicted of serious or violent felonies, or of misdemeanors that can be classified as felonies.

It was a very toxic issue and our city council got caught up in the middle of it. On May 8th, the council met to consider whether or not to file an amicus brief in support of a national lawsuit against the state of California regarding SB54. The council chambers were standing room only. The overflow room, the Century room, was also at capacity, and those who couldn't get in gathered in the parking lot. All told there were over 300 people at the meeting, and they were passionate and loud. It was a precarious situation. Before going into chambers, councilmembers were advised of the extra security measures put in place for us. That was a bit alarming. One hundred and twenty-five speakers submitted speaker cards that night. Each was allowed three uninterrupted minutes to speak. It was going to be a long night.

Mayor Laurene Weste was the right mayor at the right time. She's compassionate, fair, and very understanding. She is also a no-nonsense person who does not allow breaking with decorum and/or the rules of the chamber. She banged the gavel a number of times but overall she ran the meeting as well as anyone could have done.

When all the speakers had had their turns at the microphone, it was my turn to speak. I told those in attendance, "This is not about sanctuary cities, this is not about immigration, this is about SB54 and only SB54. It's about criminals. It's not about coming across the border illegally and people knocking at your door and pulling you out of your house and breaking up families. It's not about that. If it were about that I wouldn't be for it. It's about criminals."

I was not in favor of SB54. I was in favor of keeping felons out of our neighborhoods. If we were going to release them, release them back to their countries. Don't release them into our neighborhoods. I voted my conscience. I voted my roots, my patriotic roots, and I voted for the safety of my community. The council was unanimous in supporting the amicus brief against SB54. One of the longest meetings in council history adjourned at 1:15 a.m.

2020 Election Campaign

When I was appointed to my seat on the city council, it was only for a partial term. Now that the term was almost up I had to campaign to win the seat for another four years. Elections are crazy. You've got to raise money and you have to meet people to get their votes. I had to engage with every organization in our community. I met with businesses, non-profits, service organizations, and schools. I told them why I was running, what I had done and what I would continue to do for our community.

I put together a terrific campaign team that including dozens of people doing all the work necessary to win political campaigns. My campaign manager, Lee Watters of the Watters Group, led it, and my good friend Fred Arnold was one of my strongest supporters. They, after Virginia, were my most trusted political advisers. My main requirement of team members was that everyone genuinely loved Santa Clarita. When you love Santa Clarita you will fight for her. You will energize yourself to preserve her and all the good in her. You won't be distracted by opponents who want to change Santa Clarita and turn it into a place they came here to avoid.

My time was consumed with meeting people, raising money, and placing signs. Towards the end of the campaign, Virginia and I would sneak out in the middle of the night and put more signs up. It was fun. We felt like the older, non-criminal version of Bonnie and Clyde. By election night my team and I had done everything we needed to do to win and I was cautiously optimistic.

Election night was a little scary because until all the votes are counted, you just never know. You can go to bed in the lead and wake up to defeat. So I stayed up until 3:00 a.m. in the morning waiting. By then I had an almost 2,000 vote lead with most of the votes counted. I went to sleep feeling good about my chances.

I got up late that morning, had breakfast then opened my computer to get the results. I had won!

Willy and Ingrid Blanco Arroyo, owners of D'Wilfri DanceArt, threw us an incredible victory party that week that included dozens of our closest friends. It gave me a chance to personally thank each of my campaign team members for their contributions to our win. There was great food, outstanding music, and as always, Virginia and I danced the night away.

Eva's Cancer Diagnosis

In the middle of the summer, during my campaign, my daughter Eva was diagnosed with stage four metastasized breast cancer. She was not yet 42-years-old and the mother of three. The children were 3, 5, and 7 at the time. We were stunned. We were devastated. This daughter ran marathons. She was in great shape physically, ate healthy, exercised regularly and led a good life. She didn't smoke and only drank socially. We thought she was the picture of good health.

My first reaction was to drop out of the campaign and devote myself to supporting my daughter. Whatever she needed, I would be there for her. I was willing to stay with her and babysit the kids every day or whatever she needed. I just wanted to be there for her. Virginia and I wept together and spent some time in deep prayer before driving to see her. It was an emotional reunion. I told her that I was there for her and that I was dropping out of the race. I would be hers 24/7. But without hesitation, she grabbed a hold of me and pointed her finger within an inch of my face. "Don't you dare drop out of the campaign."

I was taken aback.

"You take care of the campaign," she insisted. "That's important. It's important to you, and it's important to me." I thought about arguing with her, but she was insistent. I went there to help, and she told me how I could help. So I

honored her wishes and halfheartedly turned my attention back to the campaign. Her words kept running over and over in my mind and at some point they began to energize me instead of weighing me down. I wasn't just running for myself. I was running for Eva, too. I needed to be busy and stay active. I needed to not overthink, or dwell on any negativity. I needed to put positive vibes out there for her, as well as for myself and everyone around us.

Eva has survived three years now. She's staying ahead of the Grim Reaper. She receives regular treatments by top-notch medical professionals. Periodically they switch her treatments as they discover new medications in an effort to stay ahead of the game. She knows that when they stop discovering new medications, it's game over.

Eva is my hero. She's handled this challenge better than I ever could have and better than anyone I know. I pray every day for her, her family, and her supporters and caregivers. I pray for all those who suffer from terminal diseases and for their families.

I am so grateful for the many people praying for and supporting my beautiful Eva that I couldn't begin to list them all by name. We are humbled by the unbelievable outpouring of love and support my family has received and Virginia and I thank all of you from the bottom of our hearts.

4th of July Parade

CHAPTER FOURTEEN

COUNCIL YEARS 3 & 4

Year Three: Disasters Strike

My third year serving on the council was filled with many things, but two were defining. The Tick Fire and the Saugus High School Shooting.

Tick Fire

The Tick Fire began the afternoon of Thursday, October 24 (2019) near Tick Canyon Road in Canyon Country. In less than a couple of hours 1,000 acres were ablaze. By the next morning, the fire had jumped the heavily traveled 14 Freeway and the road was closed. The fire covered thousands of acres and threatened thousands of homes. Governor Newsom declared a State of Emergency. Evacuation orders were issued for 15,000 homes and almost 40,000 residents. It was the largest evacuation ever in Santa Clarita.

Santa Claritans have always come together in the face of emergencies and this time was no different. Many of our residents opened their homes to evacuees. Schools and city facilities were utilized. Evacuees not only needed shelter, but they needed food, clothing, blankets and personal care items. Most importantly, they needed assurances that their lives were not destroyed.

I did my best to provide assurances to as many people as I could. I frequented the many shelters but mostly the one located on the College of the Canyons Valencia campus. They'd set up a temporary shelter in their gymnasium. The people running the shelter were on their A game. They had cots, blankets, sundry items, and food for everyone. Our local merchants donated many of the items and I couldn't thank them enough. By Monday afternoon most of the evacuation orders were lifted. Exactly one week from the start of the fire, our firefighters achieved 100 percent containment.

I can't express my gratitude enough to the thousands who helped our community survive the fire. To our brave firefighters who never gave up despite extreme temperatures, winds, and exhaustion, we owe our humble thanks. Community businesses and organizations rallied their resources and personnel to help in any way they could. Our students helped, too. They offered physical help and raised money for the victims of the fire. Little did we know, it was a dress rehearsal for what was to come.

The Saugus High School Shooting

The morning of Thursday, November 14th was one of the most tragic in Santa Clarita history. For no apparent reason, a Saugus High School student pulled out a pistol in the school courtyard and shot six people, including himself. Three off-duty police officers from various agencies that had just dropped off kids at the school, heard the shots and rushed to the courtyard. After making sure the courtyard was safe, they helped administer medical aid to the victims. They were joined shortly thereafter by our local sheriffs and firefighters. All of the injured were rushed to area hospitals.

Word of the shooting spread throughout the school like wildfire. It was an atmosphere of contained fear. The teachers and students had been trained for such emergencies. To their credit they did what they were trained to do. Teachers locked doors and in many cases barricaded them. Some students obtained scissors or other sharp objects to protect themselves if needed. Shades were drawn and lights were turned off. Many students prayed silently for help. Some cried. Others, frozen in fear, were too scared to cry. Some tried to text their parents. I can't imagine what it would be like to get a text from your child saying there was a shooter in the school. What would you say? Some texts were indecipherable because hands shook too much to text properly. Those who called and got through left messages that ended with, "I love you."

The Los Angeles Sheriff's Department deputies are trained to very carefully clear areas at a facility before beginning evacuations. Officers went hall-to-hall and door-to-door. They asked the students to follow their instructions carefully. Students were instructed to leave quickly, orderly, and show their hands at all times. They were then directed to walk or take a waiting bus to Central Park where they should wait to reunite with their loved ones.

When news of the shooting hit the community, parents panicked fearing for their children. The city, along with the Sheriff's department, fire departments, and hospitals, went into emergency mode. A command center was established at Central Park. We asked parents and students to reunite there. The injured were taken by ambulance to Henry Mayo Newhall Hospital or to Providence Holy Cross Hospital in nearby Mission Hills.

I rushed to Central Park and the Command Center. The scene at the park was extremely emotional. People were crying and shaking, hugging and praying, and trying to discern exactly what had happened. Police, including county, state, and federal officers surrounded the command center. No stone was left unturned. The situation was strictly monitored to ensure we got the facts straight and that we had, in fact, cleared all areas of potential danger.

L.A. County Sheriff Alex Villanueva held a press conference. City officials stood by his side. Dozens of news cameras faced him, waiting anxiously for details. He began, "I regret to inform you it's a sad day for Saugus, Los Angeles County, and the nation."

He reported that one student was dead, two were in critical condition, and three were in stable condition. During the press conference we were informed that a second student had died. Government officials took time to show support for the Saugus community and offer help. Mayor McLean told the gathering that when she heard the news her greatest concern was for the children. She added that her granddaughter was at the school that morning. Mayor McLean was extremely supportive of all efforts to help the families of the victims.

Tragically, by day's end, students Gracie Muehlberger and Dominic Blackwell died as a result of their wounds. The next day, the shooter succumbed to his injuries. Another student was treated and released and two students remained in stable condition. That evening, Virginia and I visited as many venues as we could to offer our support. People gathered in small groups sharing their experiences and opening themselves up by sharing their fears and deep sorrows. Mental health counselors were everywhere helping people cope the best they could. Small makeshift vigils were held throughout the city. A citywide vigil was planned for Sunday evening at Central Park. A collaboration between the city, school board, churches, and Saugus students brought the communal event together.

That Sunday evening, Virginia and I arrived at Central Park to an incredible display of support for Saugus students. Thousands of people were wearing Saugus Strong shirts and buttons. Those holding candles crowded into the park in front of a large stage where we held a 90-minute gut wrenching display of support and solidarity. There were prayers and music fitting the occasion. Loved ones, some still in shock, spoke about the departed. Mayor McLean spoke and said, "Tonight and every night, we are all Saugus Strong!"

On February 18, 2021, the words In Memoriam Gracie Muehlberger and Dominic Blackwell were added to a sign at the entrance to Central Park to honor the victims of the shooting. On June 4, 2021 a beautiful memorial consisting of two eleven-foot tall concrete and mosaic obelisks were unveiled near the entrance to Central Park. It is a fitting memorial dedicated to the memories of both Gracie and Dominic.

Year Four: Mayor Pro Tem

The Pandemic

In December of 2019 the council held its reorganization meeting and I was chosen to be the Mayor Pro Tem. Cameron Smyth became mayor again. Early in 2020 COVID-19 shook the world and it changed everything. It began with information flow. Many of our typically reliable information sources were giving us conflicting data. Governments were reacting in a variety of ways in an attempt to avoid or fight the virus. Some shut down immediately while others took a more laissez faire approach. Santa Clarita does not have its own health department, which meant we had to follow county and state health department mandates. Both called for a lock down. Almost everything closed. It was bad. Really bad.

Businesses and so-called non-essential organizations were shut down. Government buildings were limited in the number of employees and visitors they could have. Non-profit organizations were limited in their fundraising ability. Our schools, libraries, and community centers were closed.

There were business closures, job losses, economic crises, and we weren't even allowed to attend churches or visit hospitals. We lost hundreds of our citizens to the virus.

Everyone has a pandemic story much more interesting than mine, so I'll tell mine quickly. Virginia's art business was very much affected. She was forced to close her art studio, her main source of income. I had to stop my consulting business for months. Fortunately, the studio closure gave Virginia more time to paint and she was able to sell some of her paintings. Between our modest incomes we survived financially.

We did our best to help our relatives. We babysat the grandkids as much as we could as school was closed. We helped with Virginia's 98-year-old mother and Virginia's 79-year-old sister. When we were exhausted or getting claustrophobic at home, we took a field trip for two weeks up State Highway 395 to Mammoth Lakes and then on to Reno. The destinations were great, but it was the views along the way that captured our hearts. California is a beautiful state. We returned from our trips fully rested and ready to soldier on.

Ice Station Valencia Becomes The Cube

Ice Station Valencia had been around for 20 years. The ice skating rink was one of the most used facilities in Santa Clarita. The facility was already struggling to make ends meet and the pandemic finished it off. As soon as they closed the building and listed it for sale, developers lined up to buy it. They had visions of tearing down the building, developing the property and making it into something else. The council was saddened by the news, but the last thing we were thinking about was buying an ice rink in the middle of a pandemic. Here's why I think this story should be in every government textbook as an example.

The community was about to lose one of the most popular venues in our city. The citizens weren't having it. They started a grassroots movement to save the ice rink. Leigh Ann Dunleavey and Stacey Titter were two of the leaders. A petition was started that read in part:

Thousands of kids are devastated right now with the closing of their place to forget all their troubles and pursue their passion. The undersigned of this petition ask the City of Santa Clarita and the Los Angeles Kings to ensure the ice does not leave Santa Clarita. We ask these organizations to purchase and operate the rink and continue to bring joy to thousands in our local community. It will not be Awesometown without ice! Thank you for your support!

Over 26,000 people signed the petition. I can't tell you how many emails, texts, and phone calls I got from people asking, almost begging me, to advocate for the city buying the ice rink. Supporters attended the virtual council meetings by the dozens and pleaded with the council to save the rink.

At a crucial council meeting on the subject, supporters of the movement reminded us of their petition and their pleas. The council was really not of a mood to buy the rink, but they were in the mood to save the rink. At that point I felt leadership needed to step in and I was willing to lead. I did what I consider to be a very bold thing.

I addressed our City Manager. "This is akin to the loss of a park. This is akin to the loss of Meadows Park or Heritage Park or any other park. More people use the Ice Station than we can imagine. It's very heavily used. I don't understand why they ran out of money. I think that's what happened, but it is very heavily used. I had the pleasure last year with Senator Scott Wilk to drop the puck at a special needs tournament that brought tears to everybody's eyes in the arena. That can't happen if we don't have an ice rink. I know this is not a good time, City Manager, I agree with you. There's never a good time and this is quite possibly one of the worst. But this is akin to losing a park. We cannot under any circumstances lose the ice station. I feel very strongly about that."

When I said "under any circumstances" I could almost see the City Manager's head go down a bit. He's the one responsible for the budget. I think my words helped to change the council's thinking from this is not a good time, to this is something we have to do.

We voted to hire a consultant to analyze whether or not buying the rink was even viable. The consultant reported it was viable if we did certain things. The staff said they could do them and at another council meeting the council voted unanimously to purchase the rink.

To the City Manager's credit, once the council voted, he and his staff went into overdrive to help put in place plans and actions for renovation of the rink. Hopefully, someday

Assistant City Manager Frank Oviedo will write a book about all that was done to get from that night's vote to the reopening of the ice rink. It was incredible.

Shortly after the city purchased the rink, renovation not yet begun, we were all invited to a car parade outside the ice rink. A parade of many cars driven by supporters of the grassroots movement, many with their children, waved to us showing their gratitude as they drove by. I thought the parade might last ten or 15 minutes and it lasted almost an hour. Every car was filled with kids. Some people were in tears, emotional because we saved the rink. Virginia teared up, too. I tried to hold it together. Signs, decorations and flags adorned the cars. Kids and parents waved flags. I've been thanked for a lot of things in my life, but that was a thank you I'll never forget. It was just amazing.

Supporters of the rink started the movement. They expanded the movement. They made their case before the council and the council fed on their energy. We didn't create our own. The community fed on that energy. We bought the rink and completely renovated it. But it was the collective energy and commitment from everyone that made it happen.

We needed someone to run the rink, so we put out a call for bids. We awarded the contract to American Sports Entertainment Company and the LA Kings. We could not have gotten a better operator for the rink. In April 2021, we held the grand opening of the renovated and renamed rink we call The Cube. The great Hall of Fame hockey player president of the Los Angeles Kings hockey team, Luc Robitaille, attended our ribbon cutting ceremony along with many hockey celebrities. Even in the midst of the pandemic more than 100 people attended. I was honored to be the host and the emcee of the event.

Today, thousands enjoy the ice because our community saved it. And here's something else. There's an organization called SNAP (Special Needs Athletes and Peers) that uses the rink on a regular basis. Before the pandemic I stood at center ice and high-fived about 200 of those kids as they skated onto the rink for tournament play. As I stood at center ice, I looked up in the stands to see Virginia applauding, tears running down her cheeks.

These kids didn't say, "I can't do it."

These kids didn't say, "It's not the right time."

These kids said, "Yes, I can."

Who can say no to that?

The BLM Protests

In the aftermath of the May 25th murder of George Floyd, protests were held throughout the country. Millions of people protested against police brutality and systemic racism. The majority of the protests were peaceful. Unfortunately, some were not.

In early June we caught wind through social media of plans to hold a protest in Santa Clarita. There were estimates that 800 protesters from both inside and outside of the city were planning to attend. We also got word that a counter protest was being planned. We had no choice but to plan for any eventuality, especially since Los Angeles, Long Beach, and Santa Monica had some protests turn to riots. Los Angeles, one of the largest police departments in the country, had to request help from the National Guard.

Because of the potential counter protest we declared a "state of emergency," instituted a 6 p.m. curfew, and requested National Guard backup just in case they were needed. We did not anticipate a riot, but the council's primary responsibility is to keep its citizens safe and we were going to do everything in our power to ensure their safety.

The protests were peaceful. Virginia and I drove past the protesters several times just to keep an eye on things. We'd been asked by friends to join in the protest but some of the placards and signs we saw were disgusting, and for us it was totally out of the question. Virginia and I are both against bad policing, as are most people with a brain. We support open discussions on how to better train police officers to react better in situations that cause them to lose control or make bad decisions. That said, we are staunch supporters of good policing, and feel that is what we have 99% of the time. Under outstanding police captains including our current captain, Justin Diez, our sheriff station ranks as one of the best, and has helped to make Santa Clarita one of the safest cities in America. We are proud of and forever grateful to the members of our sheriff station.

The Human Relations Roundtable

As a result of the BLM protests and concerned citizens coming to us to start the conversation on racism, biases, and hate crimes in our city, Mayor Cameron Smyth and I offered to create a human relations roundtable. The table would consist of about 15 community members representing all of the major demographics in our city.

We formed a selection committee consisting of five people, influential leaders in our community. They accepted and reviewed more than 80 applications and selected 30 for personal interviews. The selection committee chose 15 people to join the roundtable. The first meeting was held in December 2020. The mission of the roundtable is to help eliminate racism in all its forms and to promote multiculturalism, diversity, equity, and inclusion in our city.

Reorganization

At the last council meeting of 2020, the council reorganized, as is its custom. Retiring Councilmember Bob Kellar received accolades for his 20 years of service on the council. Although he may have had a few hiccups along the way, I can tell you firsthand that Bob Kellar is a gentleman, a dedicated civil servant, and a lover of all things Santa Clarita and America. He deserves our gratitude.

Outgoing Mayor Cameron Smyth received his own accolades for the excellent work he did as mayor during one of the city's most trying years in its history. He and incoming Councilmember Jason Gibbs were sworn in for terms to last four years.

Lastly, the council voted me in as the new mayor. I became the 14th mayor in Santa Clarita's 33-year history. I became the first Latino and first person of color to serve as mayor of Santa Clarita. That means a great deal to many members of our community. It is a powerful symbol that gives us a view of the future of politics in our city. Santa Clarita doesn't just talk about multiculturalism, diversity, equity, and inclusion. We embrace it.

2021 New Council

L-R: Councilmember Cameron Smyth, Councilmember Marsha McLean, Mayor Bill Miranda, Mayor Pro Tem Laurene Weste, Councilmember Jason Gibbs

CHAPTER FIFTEEN

THE MAYOR YEAR

On Leadership

I bring to the mayorship a collection of unique and valuable experiences. I incorporate those experiences with an understanding, compassion, a willingness to listen, a willingness to learn, and a willingness to serve every demographic of our community. I'm your mayor and your public servant.

My goal as mayor is to work to help Santa Clarita become a leader in embracing the society of the 21st century. That society is multicultural, diverse and inclusive. That society is a melting pot of people, beliefs, and ideas. It is the future and we can get there by working together to achieve it.

My definition of leadership includes having a grand vision, communicating it clearly, and trusting our team members to help get it done. I'm about trusting and being trustworthy. If you're not trusting you won't be open to valuable input from others. If you're not trustworthy, others won't give you their input and you will fail.

Good to Great

Santa Clarita is a good city. Many more people want to move here than want to leave. We may not be perfect (what city is?), but we can still be great. I grew up in what I thought was the greatest city in the world. It was a societal melting pot and a cultural Mecca. I don't want to replicate New York, or even Los Angeles. I do want to create a much smaller, gentler version of the things that make those cities great while avoiding the things that made me want to leave them.

Let's start with an art museum, a historic museum and a cultural center. We have dozens of world-class artists right here in Santa Clarita. Why not give them a show place to showcase? Here's an idea that helps get us from good to great in a hurry. Convert the old senior center in Old Town Newhall into an art museum. We can do some renovations and have it ready to open as a wonderful art museum in the not too distant future. We have to get the county to release the empty building to us and renovate it so thousands of our citizens can enjoy it. Both the City and the County are working on making it happen.

Santa Clarita can easily showcase the history of the west on a localized level. Here is where gold was first discovered. It was in the Santa Clarita Valley at Placerita Canyon. The Pioneer Oil Refinery was the first successful oil refinery in California, built in Newhall in 1876. Since 1903, Santa Clarita has been the setting for thousands of movies and TV shows including some of the great classics. Wouldn't it be great to have a historic museum that chronicles our history to share with our children and grandchildren? How about investing in, renovating, and enlarging Heritage Junction at William S. Hart Park? This is a County owned property and the Historical Society has received funds from the City to complete renovations that are currently underway. Councilmember Laurene Weste has been at the forefront of advocating and working "hands on" to help make this happen. Everyone wants to do it. The Historical Society wants it, the schools would love it, and the city wants it. We can convert it into a true destination by investing in some site infrastructure. It can be a student-friendly place where our history is on display in a fun, interactive manner. We can do that and have a wonderful site there for thousands to enjoy. Let's do it!

What I'm most passionate about is the creation of a cultural museum. There we can highlight the histories, accomplishments and struggles of the different cultures in our community. We can teach our children the things that make for a great society. We can teach them to understand and accept our differences and value the things that make us the same. Why not annex the Tesoro Adobe and enhance it to display not only its own cultural history, but also that of the various cultures within Santa Clarita? The Latino Business Alliance wants it, the Human Relations Roundtable wants it, the Filipino American association wants it, the city wants it, and hopefully the county wants it. Let's do it!

Good to great only happens if we have the will to act. I've seen many great things started with two simple things: a clear vision and the passion to take the first step. Let's take those first steps together.

Public Safety

My first priority will always be public safety. People move to Santa Clarita for good schools in a safe environment. Recently Smart Asset named Santa Clarita the 4th safest city in the country. Maybe we are and maybe we aren't, but it sure is great to be in the conversation.

Unfortunately, two issues have potentially endangered our public safety: the LA County District Attorney's office decision not to prosecute a number of crimes is one. The moving of prisoners in the L.A. County juvenile detention centers to two locations in Santa Clarita in the middle of housing areas is the other.

We are contesting the District Attorney's actions because we feel that if we capture a criminal in the act of committing a crime, and that person is arrested and booked, that person should be charged with the crime and then have his or her day in court. We feel the D.A. should not have the authority to determine whether or not the cases should be prosecuted. We sent a letter of No Confidence to the district attorney. We were the first and there are other cities that are following suit. Hopefully, it will have an impact and the D.A. will change his mind on some of these cases.

Regarding moving detainees from the juvenile detention center in Los Angeles to Santa Clarita's Camp Scott and Camp Scudder, both are near residential areas that could present a serious danger to our citizens. I have sent a letter to the County Board of Supervisors and spoken on the issue both formally and informally with stakeholders on both sides of the issue. Our efforts have halted the immediate relocation and the county is now reviewing the situation further before a decision is made. I am certain that once the county has a chance to review their choices they will choose another location outside of our city.

Economic Vitality

Another priority is economic vitality. With a population projected to be at almost 300,000 people in our valley, we will always need jobs, jobs, and more jobs. Santa Clarita is business friendly, but with lots of rules that help businesses be community friendly, too. Let's protect our environment, open spaces, and parks, while we create jobs locally.

One of my major concerns is how are we going to continue to grow at our current rate without building more roads? The answer is we can't. I'm hoping we can get the Dockweiler Extension built in the next five years followed closely with the building of the Via Princessa Extension westward into Wiley Canyon Road. Those will help, but we will need a combination of more roads and less auto travel to have a good transportation network.

Pandemic and Reopening

Because Santa Clarita doesn't have its own health department, we are under the auspices of federal, state, and county health departments. Before anyone suggests we get our own health department, I can tell you we looked into it and determined the ridiculously high cost outweighed the potential benefits. Thus, Santa Clarita has had to abide by the other agencies' mandates. Masks, social distancing, no mass gatherings, no indoor dining, no gyms, no beauty salons, etc.

Slowly but surely in 2021 we've learned somewhat to control the pandemic and hopefully we'll defeat it. One of my jobs as mayor is to be enthusiastic and to do what I can to get our economy back up and moving. Let's get our film and hospitality industries rolling full bore again. Let's open up our entertainment centers and theaters again. We held the grand openings of the Laemmle Theatre and The Cube. Later in the year we'll open the new sheriff's station and Canyon Country Community Center. Let's keep the momentum going.

Social Justice

The Human Relations Roundtable is a positive thing. As I write this we are still trying to wrap our arms around it. It is our goal to grow it into a strong voice of advocacy for multiculturalism, diversity, equity, and inclusion. We want to ensure that our citizens feel good about what we're doing.

As I said earlier, Black Lives Matter protesters made their way to Santa Clarita in 2020. The protests were peaceful and passionate. There were issues that needed to be addressed that, frankly, the city had not addressed completely. It's easy to forget that there are minorities in the city, and that we've seen some acts of racism perpetrated against some of them. It's easy to ignore them when you have a big, wonderful city, filled with paseos, parks, recreation, and entertainment. But we cannot ignore the acts of hate no matter how infrequent. It's prudent for us to continue to work positively to progress in this area.

Injustice is injustice. Whether it takes place in New York or Los Angeles or Santa Clarita. I'm very proud of the members of the Roundtable for stepping up and for their willingness to work to help end all forms of racism in our community.

One important part of their mission is to educate our community. Early in 2021 the roundtable released two videos that I think illustrate the impact of Martin Luther King in the world and in our own community. It includes black men and women in our local history that have made a difference. It's only a start. We have to continue to do more to educate our community about race. A cultural museum will be a large step in that direction.

The Arts

Although the city offers art displays at city hall and various other small venues, it's not the same as having an art museum where artists can display their work in a manner that shows and tells their stories. All the great cities of the world have outstanding art museums. As I mentioned before, we can have one next year if we focus on making it happen.

Santa Clarita has a 2025 plan. That plan includes a cultural center. I don't want it to be one of those things that doesn't get done. I am emphatic when I say that the cultural center is critical to our community. It's how we're going to educate our students and ourselves. It will be a place where every student visits once or more a year and learns about the different cultures in our community, and why they are all valuable.

Seniors

Seniors in Santa Clarita were only able to use the new senior center, named Bella Vida, for a short time before the pandemic hit. The good news is that the team has done an excellent job of continuing their services to our seniors.

Instead of dine-in meals, seniors got to experience drive-through meals. Volunteers who ran our Meals on Wheels program delivered many more meals to those who could not drive to the center. Programs normally offered at the center such as drawing, painting, and writing were continued over zoom meetings.

Kevin MacDonald, who's the head of the senior center, and his outstanding staff of employees and volunteers, have created a fantastic outreach program for seniors. Their goal is to serve every senior in our community. They work to not only feed bellies, but minds and spirits, too. The city helps a great deal. We provided some funding for the center and recently we helped with vaccine distribution to them. We can do more. We're in the process of building the Canyon Country Community Center in a senior-friendly manner. I expect many seniors, especially those in and around Canyon Country, will enjoy the activities we have planned for them there.

Veterans & First Responders

I'm a veteran and I have been supporting veterans programs for years. I know some of what veterans experience. PTSD is only one of their travails. Joblessness and homelessness are others. Santa Clarita has a Veterans' Collaborative that helps veterans in our city. We have the American Legion and Veterans of Foreign Wars as well. Homes4Families does great work supporting our vets and their families.

This year I was introduced to a service organization called Guardians. They provide care for those who care for others. They serve veterans as well as first responders namely firefighters, police, and medical workers. They provide regular meetings where attendees can share their feelings and concerns with one another in a warm expression of love and kindness. I had the pleasure of participating in several of their meetings. They are not just about socializing. They are about giving and getting needed help. It's a terrific organization.

Homelessness

Basically there are three reasons people end up homeless: lack of mental capacity, addiction, and falling on bad economic times. The first requires mental counseling. We need to establish a mechanism where they can get the mental help they need to get well, or at least well enough to be able to function in society.

In the second group are those who are homeless due to addiction. It's a serious problem. We need a mechanism to help them detox. Just like we need to send the first group for mental counseling or mental treatment, we need to send the second group to drug rehab. It's expensive. Both of those alternatives are expensive, but if we want to solve the problem, that's what we have to do.

The third group consists of folks who've lost their jobs, can't find work, don't have the right skills, or just don't have a place to live. Folks who are just down on their luck. We need to help them, whether it's with job skills training, preparing them for the workforce or connecting them with employers.

To make a dent in the homeless problem all three must be addressed. Homelessness will never be eradicated. It's almost as old as the world. But we can make a serious dent in it here in Santa Clarita if we make the big effort. Start with a homeless shelter that has a front desk and a staff that says, "Let me help you," and then determines which of the three groups they fall under and get them the help they need.

LA County Measure H, which allocated $350 million per year to fight homelessness, was passed almost four years ago. Santa Clarita sends millions of dollars to L.A. County in sales tax revenues. We only get a fraction of it back. We don't mind helping the county at large, but we want to get a fair share of our money back. I'm wondering why I see more homeless now in and around L.A. than ever. Obviously, these people are not getting the help they really need.

Districting

One of the most important issues the council will have to address this year is the issue of districting. About a quarter of California's cities elect their councils by districts.

Each councilmember represents a district or section of the city as mapped out for them. The other cities in California, like Santa Clarita, elect their councilmembers at large. Each councilmember represents the entire city.

The stated arguments made for moving to districts are that it gives minorities a better chance of being represented on the councils. Cities that have switched over in the last five years have had mixed results at best. In some cases minorities gained seats. In other cases minorities actually lost seats due to districting.

In 2020, an attorney claiming to represent a voting group was threatening to sue us over not having ample minority representation on our council, in particular, Latino representation. The councilmember I replaced was a Latino from Canyon Country. I'm a Latino from Valencia. But that didn't matter. They want what they want and screw the rest of us.

If we had districting, how passionate would three of the councilmembers be about saving the ice rink in Valencia or building a community center in Canyon Country? I'm guessing neither of those two things would get done. How about the Arts District in Old Town Newhall or the planned library in Saugus? Those who favor districts are being somewhat disingenuous because they know councilmembers are going to represent their districts before representing the city at large.

I'm against it, and that's also why I believe every other councilmember is against it. Districting does not give the people more voice. On the contrary, it gives the people less voice. You'll vote for one councilmember every four years. Right now, you get to vote for all five of them. It's in two different elections, but at least you get to vote for all five.

The council will keep an open mind, hear all the facts, and then vote their conscience. Whatever we decide, it will be with the best interest of our community in mind.

The Support Team

Council

Success on the city council depends on the ability of all five councilmembers to get along and be able to hold open and frank discussions on issues important to the city. Disagreements, sometimes strong disagreements, do take place. But once a vote is taken and a decision is made, councilmembers move forward and respectfully continue to do the work we have been elected to do.

From the moment I joined the council, the other four members have been strong supporters. We make a good team. We hear one another out, have open discussions expressing our opinions, and then vote our consciences. We are all humble public servants. We could all make a lot more money doing other things. Instead we take less and get more by serving our community.

Staff

I'm a big picture guy. I'm not so much a down-in-the-details fella. So, I need a lot of help when it comes to getting down in the details. Thankfully, I have a wonderful staff to help me. I have a great secretary, Sherrye Ketchepaw. She and I are a team. Whatever I need, I pick up the phone and she makes it happen. Magic. Not really. She, in turn, picks up the phone and calls other staff members who help her to help me.

A mayor, as well as every councilmember, has a small army of city staff to support them. They include the City Manager, the leadership team, team members in every department of the city, and the appointed members of our commissions. To use one of my favorite adages, help is everywhere. And not just help but expert help. Our city staff consists of some of the most dedicated people I have ever met.

My Legacy

Santa Clarita has always had a very involved community. We have many non-profits that are able to do their good work because of our community volunteers and donors. We have many service clubs, Soroptimist, Zonta, and Rotary to name a few, that require their members to perform community service. We have business organizations that not only serve the business community but also serve our community in general. And we have corporations that are good neighbors that contribute their resources to help make our community a caring and sharing one.

We couldn't be a successful community without so much involvement. Santa Clarita Cares is probably our unofficial motto. I know every city cares, in one way or another, but just look at our responses to the Northridge Earthquake of 1994, or the Sand Fire of 2016, or the Tick Fire and Saugus Shootings of 2019 to see Santa Clarita in care mode. It's something that makes me very proud. What makes me even more proud is that at any time I can call on members of our community to come together for the good of everyone, regardless of race, religion or political beliefs. Change is happening and we're not done yet.

It is an honor to serve the good people of Santa Clarita. Let's continue to build on those principals and together take Santa Clarita from good to great. That is what I want my legacy as mayor to be.

Most of all, I would like my legacy to be that I inspired others to become positive in their thinking and strive to be the best they can be. I want others to be inspired by my story and get out of their comfort zones. Don't shy away from challenges. Embrace them. Don't have an endpoint. There's a whole world out there so don't limit yourself. You might be pleasantly surprised.

My message to young people is this: go out and get life experiences. Don't zero in on what your career's going to be. Don't zero in on what you want to do. Zero in on getting more life experiences. I tell them, when you graduate, don't go to work right away. Go to Europe. Go to Asia. Go to South America.

Go to a different culture. See how people live there. Get the feeling. Get the flavor. Feel the music. Taste the food. Breathe the air. Live life. There'll be plenty of time for work. There'll be plenty of time for career. Do it now that you're young. Do it now that you can do it on the cheap. Just go.

Throughout my travels in Europe I saw young people traveling with small backpacks and little money in their pockets. This is how they live over there. They get out of school and then they go and travel and live life and get life experiences. I don't mean to be melodramatic, but I'm trying to remember those days. They were wonderful days of getting life experiences. Do that first. Work will take care of itself. Career will take care of itself. And by the way, what you

252

think you want to be when you're 18, 19, 20-years-old, and what you end up becoming, chances are, they're going to be quite different.

I hope this book will be great inspiration for young people and for minority people in particular. Remember this is America. Anything and everything is possible. If you can conceive it and believe it, you can achieve it. And when you get to that point, a weight goes away and the world is your oyster, and you say, "Let's do this!" That's when life becomes really, really enjoyable.

Be a Kid Again!

Take a Family Walk on the Beach

Celebrating Our Wonderful Life Together

Made in the USA
Las Vegas, NV
15 September 2021

30355323R00154